ALL ABOUT MONEY

Compiled by Peter Potter

A BULL'S-EYE BOOK

Published by
William Mulvey Inc.
72 Park Street
New Canaan, Conn. 06840

Cover design: Ted Palmer
Format design: Louis Sardella

Library of Congress Cataloging-in-Publication Data

All About Money
"A Bull's-eye Book"

Includes index.
1. Money—Quotations, maxims, etc. I. Potter, Peter (date). II. Series: All About (New Canaan, Conn.)

PN6084.M56A44 1988 332.4 86-90382
ISBN 0-934791-02-3

Printed in the United States of America
First Edition

To
Priscilla Battis
with appreciation

Introduction

Some spend all their lives running after it. Others see it as evil. "Filthy lucre."

What's good about it? What's bad about it? How do you get it? How do you keep it? What do you do if you don't have it?

Great minds have thought about money, and talked about it, down through the centuries. Wise people of today—some rich, some poor—have also thought and talked about it.

If you have money these words should make you thoughtful—and cautious. If you don't have it—well, maybe this book will help you acquire it.

Read on. Learn. Enjoy.

Peter Potter

A

Acquiring Wealth

Aging

Almsgiving

Americans

Anxiety

Appearances

Attraction

Avarice

Acquiring Wealth

Money is so unlike every other article that I believe a man has neither a legal or a moral right to take all that he can get.

Peter Cooper

The people came to realize that wealth is not the fruit of labor but the result of organized protected robbery.

Frantz Fanon

Matters are so constituted that "nothing out of nothing" is not a truer maxim in physics than in politics; and every man who is greatly destitute of money is on that account entirely excluded from all means of acquiring it.

Henry Fielding

Who is rich? He that is content. Who is that? Nobody.

Benjamin Franklin

There are only three ways by which any individual can get wealth—by work, by gift, or by theft. And, clearly, the reason why the workers get so little is that the beggars and thieves get so much.

Henry George

Neither sultry summer, nor winter, fire, ocean, sword, can drive you from gain. You surmount every obstacle, that no other man may be richer than yourself.

Horace

Sometimes the pilgrimage from rags to riches is a journey from rage to wretchedness.

R. M. Huber

No man is any the worse off because another acquires wealth by trade, or by the exercise of a profession; on the contrary, he cannot have acquired his wealth except by benefiting others to the full extent of what they considered to be its value.

T. H. Huxley

Getting money is like digging with a needle; spending it is like water soaking into sand.

Japanese proverb

There are few ways in which a man can be more innocently employed than in getting money.

Samuel Johnson

If you cannot make money on one dollar—if you do not coax one dollar to work hard for you, you won't know how to make money out of one hundred thousand dollars.

E. S. Kinnear

Making a lot of money is all right, provided you don't have to pay too much for it.

Albert Lasker

No man in this world, however high may be his rank, great his wealth, powerful his genius, or extensive his requirements, can ever attain more than health, enjoyment and respect.

J. C. Loudon

If you want to get rich from writing, write the sort of thing that's read by persons who move their lips when they're reading to themselves.

Don Marquis

The writer must earn money in order to be able to live and to write, but he must by no means live and write for the purpose of making money.

Karl Marx

What most people don't seem to realize is that there is just as much money to be made out of the wreckage of a civilization as from the upbuilding of one.

Margaret Mitchell

After a certain point money is meaningless. It ceases to be the goal. The game is what counts.

Aristotle Onassis

You can get money if you want it. You can get whatever you want. It's called 'effort'. It doesn't take much—just a lot of guts, in which the majority of the general public seem to be lacking.

Johnny Rotten

Mankind's one objective is to amass wealth.

Pascal

Ill-gotten, ill-spent.

Plautus

An object in possession seldom retains the same charm that it had in pursuit.

Pliny the Younger

Get Place and Wealth, if possible with grace;
If not, by any means get Wealth and Place.

Alexander Pope

Do you wish to become rich? You may become so if you desire it in no half-way, but thoroughly. Do you wish to master any science or accomplishment? Give yourself to it and it lies beneath your feet. This world is given as the prize for the men in earnest; and that which is true of this world, is truer still of the world to come.

Frederick William Robertson

My boy . . . always try to rub up against money, for if you rub up against money long enough, some of it may rub off on you.

Damon Runyon

The art of becoming "rich", in the common sense, is not absolutely nor finally the art of accumulating much money for ourselves, but also of contriving that our neighbors shall have less. In accurate terms, it is "the art of establishing the maximum inequality in our own favour." . . . Perhaps the final outcome and consummation of all wealth is in the producing as many as possible full-breathed, bright-eyed, and happy-hearted human creatures. Our modern wealth, I think, has rather a tendency the other way.

John Ruskin

Sudden money is going from zero to two hundred dollars a week. The rest doesn't count.

Neil Simon

You become well-to-do from doing what you do well.

Frank Tyger

Get all you can without hurting your soul, your body, or your neighbor. Save all you can, cutting off every needless expense. Give all you can. Be glad to give, and ready to distribute; laying up in store for yourselves a good foundation against the time to come, that you may attain eternal life.

John Wesley

Aging

All the precious gifts which nature had lavished on him he valued chiefly for what they would fetch. At twenty he made money of his beauty and vigor. At sixty he made money of his genius and his glory.

Thomas B. Macaulay

If a man runs after money, he's money-mad; if he keeps it, he's a capitalist; if he spends it, he's a playboy; if he doesn't get it, he's a ne'er-do-well; if he doesn't try to get it, he lacks ambition. If he gets it without working for it, he's a parasite; and if he accumulates it after a lifetime of hard work, people call him a fool who never got anything out of life.

Vic Oliver

For millions, the retirement dream is in reality an economic nightmare. For millions, growing old today means growing poor, being sick, living in substandard housing, and having to scrimp merely to subsist. And this is the prospect not only for the one out of every ten Americans now over sixty-five . . . but also for the sixty-five million who will reach retirement age within the next thirty-three years.

Sylvia Porter

Almsgiving

The bread that you store up belongs to the hungry; the cloak that lies in your chest belongs to the naked; and the gold that you have hidden in the ground belongs to the poor.

Saint Basil

Blessed is he that considereth the poor.

The Bible

He that hath pity upon the poor lendeth unto the Lord.

The Bible

When thou doest alms, let not thy left hand know what thy right hand doeth.

The Bible

Giving is a joy if we do it in the right spirit. It all depends on whether we think of it as "What can I spare?" or as "What can I share?"

Esther York Burkholder

Do not tell me of my obligation to put all poor men in good situations. Are they my poor? I tell thee, thou foolish philanthropist, that I grudge the dollar, the dime, the cent I give to such men as do not belong to me and to whom I do not belong.

Ralph Waldo Emerson

If it is more blessed to give than to receive, then most of us are content to let the other fellow have the greater blessing.

Shailer Mathews

Beggars should be abolished. It annoys one to give to them, and it annoys one not to give to them.

F. W. Nietzsche

I do not give alms; I am not poor enough for that.

F. W. Nietzsche

Feel for others—in your pocket.

Charles Haddon Spurgeon

Americans

The entire essence of America is the hope to first make money—then make money with money—then make lots of money with lots of money.

Paul Erdman

You can't appreciate home till you've left it, money till it's spent, your wife till she's joined a women's club, not Old Glory till you see it hanging on a broomstick on the shanty of a consul in a foreign town.

O. Henry

Americans relate all effort, all work, and all of life itself to the dollar. Their talk is of nothing but dollars. The English seldom sit happily chatting for hours on end about pounds. In England, public business is its own reward, nobody would go into Parliament in order to become rich, neither do riches bring public appointments.

Nancy Mitford

(Dollar) That great object of universal devotion throughout our land.

Washington Irving

Americans want action for their money. They are fascinated by its self-reproducing qualities if it's put to work . . . Gold-hoarding goes against the American grain; it fits in better with European pessimism than with America's traditional optimism.

Paula Nelson

European society . . . automatically assumes its superiority to Americans whether they have money or not, but money tends to blur the sharpness of the distinction.

Virgilia Peterson

In Hollywood the favorite word is "sex"; in the Midwest it is "cheese"; in the South, "honey"; in Manhattan, "money."

Amy Vanderbilt

Anxiety

There are more things in life to worry about than just money—how to get hold of it, for example.

Anonymous

So long as external things are sought or possessed only in a small quantity, and as much as is required for a mere livelihood, such care does not hinder one much, and consequently is not inconsistent with the perfection of Christian life . . . Yet the possession of much wealth increases the weight of care, which is a great distraction to man's mind and hinders him from giving himself wholly to God's service.

Thomas Aquinas

The sleep of a labouring man is sweet, whether he eat little or much: but the abundance of the rich will not suffer him to sleep.

The Bible

Thousands upon thousands are yearly brought into a state of real poverty by their great anxiety not to be thought poor.

William Cobbett

There is a burden of care in getting riches; fear in keeping them; temptation in using them; guilt in abusing them; sorrow in losing them; and a burden of account at last to be given concerning them.

M. Henry

(Riches are) a mind released from anxious thoughts.

William Cowper

In all recorded history there has not been one economist who has had to worry about where the next meal would come from.

Peter Drucker

(Riches are) not the end, but only a change of worries.

Epicurus

If your desires be endless, your cares and fears will be so too.

Thomas Fuller

(Money) ranks with love as man's greatest source of joy. And it ranks with death as his greatest source of anxiety. It differs from an automobile, a mistress, and cancer in being equally important to those who have it and those who don't. So when you watch people in a supermarket, you're seeing people in touch with their deepest emotions.

John Kenneth Galbraith

I am not fond of money, or anxious about it. But, though every day makes me less and less eager for wealth, every day shows me more and more strongly how necessary a competence is to a man who desires to be either great or useful.

Thomas B. Macaulay

To have money is a fear; not to have it, a grief.

George Herbert

The more you get, the more you want.

Horace

Riches do not bring freedom from sorrow and are of no avail for eternal happiness, but rather are obstacles.

Pope Leo XIII

I don't like money actually, but it quiets my nerves.

Joe Louis

Worry: the interest paid by those who borrow trouble.

George W. Lyon

But wealth is a great means of refinement; and it is a security for gentleness, since it removes disturbing anxieties.

Donald G. Mitchell

So, Money, it is you who are responsible for life's anxieties; you who force us to take the road to early death; you who foster and encourage man's vices; the seeds of ambition spring from your stock.

Propertius

There is nothing so degrading as the constant anxiety about one's means of livelihood . . .

William Somerset Maugham

(Money is) something that is more troublesome to watch than forget.

Adapted from Michel de Montaigne

You, O money, are the cause of a restless life. Because of you we journey toward a premature death; you provide cruel nourishment for the evils of men; the seed of our cares sprouts from your head.

Propertius

I know at last what distinguishes men from animals: financial worries.

Jules Renard

The only thing wealth does for some people is to make them worry about losing it.

Comte de Rivarol

For no one is worthy of a god unless he has paid no heed to riches. I am not, mind you, against your possessing them, but I want to ensure that you possess them without tremors; and this you will only achieve in one way, by convincing yourself that you can live a happy life even without them, and by always regarding them as being on the point of vanishing.

Seneca

Poor and content is rich and rich enough,
But riches fineless is as poor as winter
To him that ever fears he shall be poor.

Shakespeare

Appearances

If you aren't rich, you should always look useful.

Louis Ferdinand Celine

Keeping your clothes well pressed will keep you from looking hard pressed.

Coleman Cox

It is not poverty so much as pretense that harasses a ruined man—the struggle between a proud mind and an empty purse—the keeping up of a hollow show that must soon come to an end.

Washington Irving

When my maid packed my bags, she said, "Madame, some of these evening dresses have gone to Palm Beach with you three times." I'm hoping nobody will remember.

The Duchess of Windsor

There's too many folks of limited means who think that nothing's too good for them.

Kin Hubbard

Queen Cash gives birth and beauty.

Horace

It must be great to be rich and let the other fellow keep up appearances.

Kin Hubbard

God makes, and apparel shapes: but it's money that finishes the man.

Thomas Fuller

(Money is) a metal shoe elevator for small people to make them look as tall as others.

Moritz Saphir

He had so much money that he could afford to look poor.

Edgar Wallace

Attraction

Riches attract the attention, consideration, and congratulations of mankind.

John Adams

Money may be a curse, but you can always find sometime to take the curse off you.

Anonymous

If this man had not twelve thousand a year, he would be a very stupid fellow.

Jane Austen

He who has made his "pile" will be famous, brave and just.

Horace

It is true that money attracts; but much money repels.

Cynthia Ozick

To have money is to be virtuous, honest, beautiful and witty. And to be without is to be ugly and boring and stupid and useless.

Jean Giraudoux

Sir, money, money, the most charming of all things—money, which will say more in one moment than the most eloquent lover can in years. Perhaps you will say a main is not young; I answer, he is rich, he is not genteel, handsome, witty, brave, good-humored, but he is rich, rich, rich, rich, rich—that one word contradicts everything you can say against him.

Henry Fielding

Avarice

The miser is another man who can't seem to distinguish between his need and his greed.

Anonymous

There are more important things in life than a little money, and one of them is a lot of money.

Anonymous

Just as soon as people make enough money to live comfortably, they want to live extravagantly.

Anonymous

The true way to gain much is never to desire to gain too much. He is not rich that possesses much, but he that covets no more; and he is not poor that enjoys little, but he that wants too much.

Beaumont

Covetousness, as denoting a special sin, is called the root of all sins, in likeness to the root of a tree, in furnishing sustenance to the whole tree. For we see that by riches man acquires the means of committing any sin whatever, and of sating his desire for any sin whatever, since money helps man to obtain all manner of temporal goods. . . . So that in this sense desire for riches is the root of all sins.

Saint Thomas Aquinas

He that maketh haste to be rich shall not be innocent.

The Bible

He heaps up his money in his heart where the heart-beats can count it.

Elias Canetti

He . . . knew now, more than ever, that money was everything, the wall that stood between all he loathed and all he wanted.

Willa Cather

I knew once a very covetous, sordid fellow who used to say, "Take care of the pence, for the pounds will take care of themselves."

Lord Chesterfield

The covetous man is always poor.

Claudian

Those who seek money as a great thing, with immense solicitude, and upon it establish the especial defense of life . . . have fashioned for themselves too many gods.

Desiderius Erasmus

Material riches are proving inadequate and are depreciated. God's love is bestowing sufficient benefits on the nation and the world, but the benefits are not getting to the people. Something is intervening, and it is the greed of people. The only values that are everlasting are spiritual, and when we lose them we lose everything.

Anthony H. Evans

Greed is a bottomless pit which exhausts the person in an endless effort to satisfy the need without ever reaching satisfaction.

Erich Fromm

He who has enough to satisfy his wants, and nevertheless ceaselessly labors to acquire riches, either in order to obtain a higher social position, or that subsequently he may have enough to live without labor, or that his sons may become men of wealth and importance—all such are incited by a damnable avarice, sensuality and pride.

Henry of Langenstein

Watch out when you're getting all you want; fattening hogs ain't in luck.

Joel Chandler Harris

Avarice or the desire of gain, is a universal passion, which operates at all times, at all places, and upon all persons.

David Hume

As riches grow, care follows, and a thirst
For more and more.

Horace

Let him who has enough wish for nothing more.

Horace

He who is greedy is always in want; maintain a fixed limit to your desires.

Horace

Silver hidden in the greedy earth does not gleam.

Horace

Wealth breeds a pleurisy, ambition a fever, liberty a vertigo, and poverty a palsy.

Irish proverb

We're all born brave, trusting and greedy, and most of us remain greedy.

Mignon McLaughlin

One of the weaknesses of our age is our apparent inability to distinguish our needs from our greeds.

Don Robinson

Avarice implies a desire for money which no wise man covets.

Sallust

Wealth is like sea-water; the more we drink the thirstier we become; and the same is true of fame.

Schopenhauer

It is not the man who has little, but he who desires more, that is poor.

Seneca

If you would make a man happy, do not add to his possessions but subtract from his desires.

Seneca

More wealth, more avarice.

Italian proverb

We risk all in being too greedy.

Jean de La Fontaine

No man is poor who does not think himself so; but if, in a full fortune, with impatience he desires more, he proclaims his wants and his beggarly condition.

Jeremy Taylor

Avarice, in wanting to gain everything, loses all.

Jean de La Fontaine

People will buy anything that's one to a customer.

Sinclair Lewis

Excess of wealth is cause of covetousness.

Christopher Marlowe

Money is the alienated essence of man's work and existence; this essence dominates him and he worships it.

Karl Marx

Money destroys human roots wherever it is able to penetrate, by turning desire for gain into the sole motive. It easily manages to outweigh all other motives, because the effort it demands of the mind is so very much less. Nothing is so clear and so simple as a row of figures.

Simone Weil

B

Banks, Bankers

Bargains, Bargaining

Behavior

Borrowing

Bribery

Budget, Personal

Banks, Bankers

If you owe a bank enough money you own it.

Anonymous

The Dealers in money have always, since the days of Moses, been the dangerous class.

Peter Cooper

Foundations of a new religion can be laid only with the blessing of bankers.

Salvador Dali

A bank is a place where they lend you an umbrella in fair weather and ask for it back again when it begins to rain.

Robert Frost

The marvel of banks in relation to money—the wonder of creating deposits or issuing notes—is suspended on one silken thread. The requirement is that depositors or noteholders come in decently small numbers for the hard currency that the bank is under its obligation to pay. If all come at once, the bank cannot pay. When the thought spreads that the bank cannot pay, then, often in much haste, all come. When that occurs, the deposits or notes serving previously as money cease to be available.

John Kenneth Galbraith

Banking may well be a career from which no man really recovers.

John Kenneth Galbraith

Banking establishments are more dangerous than standing armies.

Thomas Jefferson

Banks are here to help the people who want to come up in the world.

David Rockefeller

Banks and riches are chains of gold, but still chains.

Edmund Ruffin

A banker without money is like a doctor without pills.

George Woods

Bargains, Bargaining

Make your bargain before beginning to plough.

Arab proverb

Life is the greatest bargain, we get it for nothing.

Yiddish proverb

There are very honest people who do not think that they have had a bargain unless they have cheated a merchant.

Anatole France

One of the difficult tasks in this world is to convince a woman that even a bargain costs money.

Edgar Watson Howe

Behavior

My Lady . . . had yet to learn that money cannot buy refinement of nature, that rank does not always confer nobility, and that true breeding makes itself felt in spite of external drawbacks.

Louisa May Alcott

Another advantage of being rich is that all your faults are called eccentricities.

Anonymous

Not a single outstanding teacher of moral wisdom has failed to warn that riches tend to isolate their owners, make them petty, vulnerable, a little ridiculous.

Bernard Iddings Bell

Money is always on the brain so long as there is a brain in reasonable order.

Samuel Butler

He that is poor, all his kindred scorn him; he that is rich, all are kind to him.

Thomas Fuller

There are a handful of people whom money won't spoil, and we count ourselves among them.

Mignon McLaughlin

Money—in its absence we are coarse; in its presence we are vulgar.

Mignon McLaughlin

His money corrects his judgment: he keeps his mind in his wallet.

Molière

People don't call you mad or eccentric if you are well-heeled. It's only when you're poor that they call you a nut.

Tony Randall

Who in his pocket hath no money,
In his mouth he must have honey.

Rowland Watkins

To suppose as we all suppose, that we could be rich and not behave as the rich behave, is like supposing that we could drink all day and stay sober.

Logan Pearsall Smith

Starting out to make money is the greatest mistake in life. Do what you feel you have a flair for doing, and if you are good enough at it the money will come.

Lord Rootes

The dog will dance for money.

Spanish proverb

Borrowing

Those who despise money will eventually sponge on their friends.

Chinese proverb

It saves a lot of trouble if, instead of having to earn money and save it, you can just go and borrow it.

Winston Churchill

If you would know the value of money, go and try to borrow some.

Benjamin Franklin

When debtors once have borrowed all we have to lend, they are very apt to grow shy of their creditors' company.

John VanBrugh

The human species is composed of two distinct races: the men who borrow and the men who lend.

Charles Lamb

A habit of debt is very injurious to the memory.

Austin O'Malley

Before borrowing from a friend, decide which you need more.

Addison H. Hallock

Bribery

There are poor men in this country who cannot be bought: the day I found that out, I sent my gold abroad.

Comtesse de Voigrand

Men are more often bribed by their loyalties and ambitions than by money.

Robert H. Jackson

Money is good for bribing yourself through the inconveniences of life.

Gottfried Reinhardt

Budget, Personal

When I get a little money, I buy books; and if any is left, I buy food and clothes.

Desiderius Erasmus

A budget tells us what we can't afford, but it doesn't keep us from buying it.

William Feather

Never ask of money spent
Where the spender thinks it went.

Robert Frost

The real superstar is a man or a woman raising six kids on $150 a week.

Spencer Haywood

There's too blamed many ways to spend money and not enough new ways to get it.

Kin Hubbard

Your economy, I suppose, begins now to be settled; your expenses are adjusted to your revenue, and all your people in their proper places. Resolve not to be poor: whatever you have, spend less. Poverty is a great enemy to human happiness; it certainly destroys liberty, and it makes some virtues impracticable, and others extremely difficult.

Samuel Johnson

I'm living so far beyond my income that we may almost be said to be living apart.

Hector Hugh Munro

The average family exists only on paper and its average budget is a fiction, invented by statisticians for the convenience of statisticians . . . There is no sense in attempting to fit into a ready-to-wear financial pattern which ignores your own personal wants and desires.

Sylvia Porter

I've got all the money I'll ever need if I die by four o'clock.

Henny Youngman

C

Charity (Giving)

Charity (Love)

Churches

Comfort

Competition

Convenience

Corruption

Costliness

Counsel

Creativity

Credit, Creditors

Crime

Charity (Giving)

A man may bestow great sums on the poor and indigent without being charitable, and may be charitable when he is not able to bestow anything.

Joseph Addison

Money is like mulch—not good unless it be spread.

Francis Bacon

In this world it is not what we take up, but what we give up, that makes us rich.

Henry Ward Beecher

Let everyone give as his heart tells him, neither grudgingly nor under compulsion, for God loves the man who gives cheerfully. After all, God can give you everything that you need, so that you may always have sufficient both for yourselves and for giving away to other people.

The Bible

One thing thou lackest: go thy way, sell whatsoever thou hast, and give to the poor, and thou shalt have treasure in heaven; and come, take up the cross, and follow me.

The Bible

He that hath two coats, let him impart to him that hath none; and he that hath meat, let him do likewise.

The Bible

Sell your possessions and give to the poor. Provide purses for yourselves that will not wear out, a treasure in heaven that will not be exhausted.

The Bible

Blessed is he that considereth the poor.

The Bible

If someone who is supposed to be a Christian has money enough to live well, and sees a brother in need, and won't help him—how can God's love be within him?

The Bible

It is more blessed to give than to receive.

The Bible

God loveth a cheerful giver.

The Bible

He hath riches sufficient, who hath enough to be charitable.

Thomas Browne

He who bestows his good upon the poor,
Shall have as much again, and ten times more.

John Bunyan

A man there was, and they called him mad; the more he gave, the more he had.

John Bunyan

We make a living by what we get, but we make a life by what we give.

Winston Churchill

One must be poor to know the luxury of giving.

George Eliot

God has given us two hands—one for receiving and the other for giving.

Billy Graham

They who give have all things; they who withhold have nothing.

Hindu proverb

Money spent on ourselves may be a millstone about the neck; spent on others it may give us wings like eagles.

Raymond Hitchcock

There can be no greater argument to a man of his own power than to find himself able not only to accomplish his own desires, but also to assist other men in theirs; and this is that conception wherein consisteth charity.

Thomas Hobbes

(Riches are) not . . . possession of much, but giving much.

John Chrysostom

A glad giver has but little heed of the thing that he gives, but all his desire and intent is to please and solace him to whom he gives.

Lady Julian of Norwich

Let us give according to our incomes, lest God make our incomes match our gifts.

Peter Marshall

It is incumbent on the rich to help the poor. Those who give of their substance to Christ in the person of His poor will receive a most bountiful reward when He shall come to judge the world. Those who act to the contrary will pay the penalty.

Pope Pius XI

He gives twice who gives quickly.

Publius Mimus

If thou art rich, then show the greatness of thy fortune; or what is better, the greatness of thy soul, in the meekness of thy conversation; condescend to men of low estate, support the distressed, and patronize the neglected. Be great.

Lawrence Sterne

A clergyman wrote to a wealthy and influential businessman requesting a subscription to a worthy charity and soon received a curt refusal which ended, "As far as I can see, this Christian business is just one continuous give, give, give." Replied the clergyman, "I wish to thank you for the best definition of the Christian life I have yet heard."

W.F.A. Stride

The man who leaves money to charity in his will is only giving away what no longer belongs to him.

Voltaire

Charity (Love)

Charity, like nature, abhors a vacuum. Next to putting it into the bank, men like to squander their superfluous wealth on those to whom it is sure of doing the least possible good.

William Hazlitt

Though I speak with the tongues of men and of angels, and have not charity, I am become as sounding brass, or a tinkling cymbal.

The Bible

Charity is the sterilized milk of human kindness.

Oliver Herford

Though I have all faith, so that I could remove mountains, and have not charity, I am nothing.

The Bible

Put on charity, which is the bond of perfectness.

The Bible

Now abideth faith, hope, and charity, these three; but the greatest of these is charity.

The Bible

When thou cuttest down thine harvest in thy field, and hast forgot a sheaf in the field, thou shalt not go again to fetch it: it shall be for the stranger, for the fatherless, and for the widow: that the Lord thy God may bless thee in all the work of thine hands.

The Bible

Charity suffereth long and is kind; charity envieth not; charity vaunteth not itself, is not puffed up.

The Bible

Preferring to store her money in the stomachs of the needy rather than hide it in a purse . . .

Saint Jerome

He is truly great who hath a great charity.

Thomas à Kempis

Every good act is charity. Your smiling in your brother's face, is charity; an exhortation of your fellowman to virtuous deeds, is equal to alms-giving, your putting a wanderer in the right road, is charity; your assisting the blind, is charity; your removing stones, and thorns, and other obstructions from the road, is charity; your giving water to the thirsty, is charity. A man's true wealth hereafter, is the good he does in this world to his fellowman. When he dies, people will say, "What property has he left behind him?" But the angels will ask, "What good deeds has he sent before him?"

Mahomet

An American journalist in China watched a Sister cleaning the gangrenous sores of wounded soldiers. "I wouldn't do that for a million dollars!" the visitor remarked. Without pause in her work, the Sister replied, "Neither would I."

Maryknoll Magazine

For too many giving is occasional, spasmodic, ill-proportioned. It depends on what is left over when other things have had their full share. Sometimes what it means is that only the small change lying in their pockets goes to the support of good and worthy causes.

Robert J. McCracken

Charity shall cover the multitude of sins.

The Bible

With one hand he put
A penny in the urn of poverty,
And with the other took a shilling out.

Robert Pollock

Make gifts of money and, very soon, you will find yourself in chains.

Jean Jacques Rousseau

Churches

The church is the only business that picks up during bad times.

Charles Angel

Funny how a dollar can look so big when you take it to church, and so small when you take it to the store.

Frank Clark

The poor may inherit the earth, but it will appear that the rich will inherit the church.

James A. Pike

All the riches of the world and the glory of creation, compared with the wealth of God, are extreme and abject poverty.

Saint John of the Cross

Comfort

Rich or poor, it's nice to have money.

Anonymous

I have mental joys and mental health,
Mental friends and mental wealth,
I've a wife that I love and that loves me;
I've all but riches bodily.

William Blake

To possess one small fragment of the world's surface to have a hut, a cabin or a cottage that was verily my own, to eat the fruits of my own labour on the soil—this seemed to me the crown and goal of all human felicity.

W. J. Dawson

Wealth in the home; comfortable circumstances.

Thomas Fuller

Contentment consists not in adding more fuel, but in taking away some fire; not in multiplying of wealth, but in subtracting men's desires.

Thomas Fuller

I wish I were either rich enough or poor enough to do a lot of things that are impossible in my present comfortable circumstances.

Don Herold

There's nothing so comfortable as a small bank roll; a big one is always danger.

Wilson Mizner

Money never remains just coins and pieces of paper. It is constantly changing into the comforts of daily life. Money can be translated into the beauty of living, a support in misfortune, an education, or future security. It also can be translated into a source of bitterness.

Sylvia Porter

If greater peace and better temper are found in cabins than in palaces, it is because comfort is more uncommon in the palace than it is in the cabin. Amidst all their wealth the unfortunates do not know how to live!

E. P. de Senancour

He that is not content in poverty would not be so neither in plenty; for the fault is not in the thing, but in the mind. If he be sickly, remove him from a cottage to a palace, he is at the same pass; for he carries his disease along with him. What can be happier than that condition both of mind and of fortune from which we cannot fall? A man may lie as warm and as dry under a thatched as under a gilded roof.

Seneca

Only the rich preach content to the poor.

Holbrook Jackson

Competition

(Money is) what you'd get on beautifully without if only other people weren't so crazy about it.

Margaret Harriman

S'pose you got a job a work and there's jus' one fella wants the job. You got to pay 'im what he asts. But s'pose they's a hundred men wants that job. S'pose them men got kids an' them kids is hungry. S'pose a nickel 'll buy at leas' sompin for the kids. An' you got a hundred men. Jus' offer 'em a nickel—why, they'll kill each other fightin' for that nickel.

John Steinbeck

Convenience

I had the pay phone installed in my (country) place because I knew that guests preferred it that way. It saved them the trouble of settling with me afterward, or of attempting to pay for their phone calls. It saved them trouble. And yet a spate of letters and cartoons resulted. You might have thought I was pathologically inclined, instead of taking a simple, rational step.

J. Paul Getty

The art of life is to be so well known at a good restaurant that you can pay with a check.

E. V. Lucas

Corruption

Come away! Poverty's catching.

Aphra Behn

What is got over the Devil's back will be spent under his belly.
English proverb

Morals today are corrupted by our worship of riches.

Cicero

Money is only corrupting to people who have not been corrupted or who have not learnt to make good use of it.

Olga Deterding

I don't deny that there is sin in the peasants too. And the fire of corruption is spreading visibly, hourly, working from above downwards. The spirit of isolation is coming upon the people too. Money-lenders and devourers of the commune are rising up.

Fyodor Dostoevsky

No public man can be just a little crooked.

Herbert Hoover

Filty Lucre.

The Bible

Great wealth always supports the party in power, no matter how corrupt it may be. It never exerts itself for reform, for it instinctively fears change.

Henry George

Ill fares the land, to hastening ills a prey,
Where wealth accumulates, and men decay.

Oliver Goldsmith

If a man of this world is attracted by things of this world and is estranged from his Creator, he is corrupted and he can corrupt the entire world along with him.

Moses Luzzato

He that serves God for money will serve the Devil for better wages.

Roger L'Estrange

O Lord! the sin
Done for the things there's money in.

John Masefield

Wealth tends to corrupt the mind and to nourish its love of power, and to stimulate its oppression.

Gouverneur Morris

Riches are a cause of evil, not because, of themselves, they do any evil, but because they goad men on to evil.

Posidenius

It is one of the misfortunes of the rich to be cheated on all sides; what wonder they think ill of mankind! It is riches that corrupt men, and the rich are rightly the first to feel the defects of the only tool they know. Everything is ill-done for them, except what they do themselves, and they do next to nothing.

Jean Jacques Rousseau

Money lays waste cities; it sets men to roaming from home; it seduces and corrupts honest men and turns virtue to baseness; it teaches villainy and impiety.

Sophocles

Costliness

What you get free costs too much.

Jean Anouilh

Nothing that costs only a dollar is worth having.

Elizabeth Arden

Sometimes one pays most for the things one gets for nothing.

Albert Einstein

Money often costs too much.

Ralph Waldo Emerson

When the anger of the gods is incurred, wealth or power only bring more devastating punishment.

Euripides

Christmas brings out the best in all of us, but it's tiring and expensive.

William Feather

I've come to realize that as soon as you get rich and famous, you stop picking up the bills. And as long as you're poor and struggling, you have to pay for everything.

Amanda Lear

At its present cost, life is worth about thirty cents on the dollar.

Don Herold

There's no such thing as a free lunch.

Milton Friedman

I think some folks are foolish to pay what it costs to live.

Kin Hubbard

Very cheap is very dear.

G. E. Lessing

At the devil's booth are all things sold,
Each ounce of dross costs its ounce in gold.

James Russell Lowell

Nothing is cheap which is superfluous, for what one does not need, is dear at a penny.

Plutarch

If you have to ask how much it costs, you can't afford it.

J.P. Morgan

We often buy money very much too dear.

W. M. Thackeray

All good things are cheap: all bad very dear.

Thoreau

The cost of living is going up and the chance of living is going down.

Flip Wilson

Counsel

The greatest luxury of riches is, that they enable you to escape so much good advice. The rich are always advising the poor, but the poor seldom venture to return the compliment.

Arthur Helps

Only one fellow in ten thousand understands the currency question, and we meet him every day.

Kin Hubbard

Don't offer me advice, give me money!

Spanish proverb

No man will take counsel, but every man will take money; therefore money is better than counsel.

Jonathan Swift

I wish to become rich, so that I can instruct the people and glorify honest poverty a little, like those kind-hearted, fat, benevolent people do.

Mark Twain

Creativity

(Money is) the commonest of our talents.

William Gibson

To have subsidized a Bach, or Fulbrighted a Beethoven would have done no good at all. Money may kindle but it cannot by itself, and for very long, burn.

Igor Stravinsky

Benjamin Franklin may have discovered electricity—but it was the man who invented the meter who made the money.

Earl Wilson

Credit, Creditors

With a credit card, you don't need money; and with money, you don't need a credit card.

Anonymous

The problem nowadays is not so much how to live within your income, but how to live within your credit.

Anonymous

Ever since the introduction of installment credit plans, people have been wishing they could afford to live the way they are living.

Anonymous

Money isn't everything, but it's might handy if you don't have a credit card.

Anonymous

Money can't buy happiness—that's why we have credit cards.

Anonymous

Credit is a clever financial trick that enables us to spend what we haven't got.

Anonymous

Money is the poor people's credit card.

Marshall McLuhan

Creditors are a superstitious sect, great observers of set days and times.

Benjamin Franklin

Getting along with women,
Knocking around with men,
Having more credit than money,
Thus one goes through the world.

Johann W. von Goethe

No man's credit is as good as his money.

Ed Howe

The creditor hath a better memory than the debtor.

James Howell

The rich are different from you and me because they have more credit.

John Leonard

Credit buying is much like being drunk. The buzz happens immediately, and it gives you a lift. . . . The hangover comes the day after.

Joyce Brothers

A credit card is a money tool, not a supplement to money. The failure to make this distinction has "supplemented" many a poor soul right into bankruptcy.

Paula Nelson

Good people, hark ye: A few rules well observed, will contribute much to your happiness and independence. Never buy what you do not really want. Never purchase on credit what you can possibly do without. Take pride in being able to say, I owe no man.

Poor Robert

Pay as you go, but not if you intend going for good.

James Jeffrey Roche

The surest way to establish your credit is to work yourself into the position of not needing any.

Switzer

Nowadays people can be divided into three classes—the Haves, the Have-Nots, and the Have-Not-Paid-For-What-They-Haves.

Earl Wilson

Crime

It is no secret that organized crime in America takes in over forty billion dollars a year. This is quite a profitable sum, especially when one considers that the Mafia spends very little for office supplies.

Woody Allen

It is harder for a rich man to enter heaven—or jail.

Anonymous

I have always thought it would be easier to redeem a man steeped in vice and crime than a greedy, narrow-minded, pitiless merchant.

Albert Camus

He who wishes to be rich in a day will be hanged in a year.

Leonardo da Vinci

There are no new forms of financial fraud; in the last several hundred years, there have only been small variations on a few classic designs.

John Kenneth Galbraith

Prefer loss to the wealth of dishonest gain; the former vexes you for a time; the latter will bring you lasting remorse.

Chilo

D

Death
Dignity
Distribution

Death

It is not earthly riches which makes us or our sons happy; for they must either be lost by us in our lifetime; or be possessed when we are dead, by whom we know not, or perhaps by whom we would not.

Saint Augustine

It costs a lot of money to die comfortably.

Samuel Butler

The man who dies rich dies disgraced.

Andrew Carnegie

True, you can't take it with you, but then, that's not the place where it comes in handy.

Brendan Francis

If your riches are yours, why don't you take them with you to t'other world.

Benjamin Franklin

Death is the poor man's Doctor.

German proverb

If the rich could hire other people to die for them, the poor could make a wonderful living.

Jewish proverb

Man enters the world with closed hands, as if to say: "The world is mine". He leaves it with open hands, as if to say: "Behold, I take nothing with me."

The Midrash

It's no great step for a poor man to the grave.
He's lived his life out only half-alive.
But when the man of plenty nears the end of his,
Death yawns beneath him like a precipice.

Palladas

There's no reason to be the richest man in the cemetery. You can't do any business from there.

Colonel Sanders

Dignity

I've been struck all my life in our great people by their dignity, their true and seemly dignity. I've seen it myself, I can testify to it, I've seen it and marvelled at it, I've seen it in spite of the degraded sins and poverty-stricken appearance of our peasantry.

Fyodor Dostoyevsky

As favour and riches forsake a man, we discover in him the foolishness they concealed, and which no-one perceived before.

Jean de La Bruyère

A servant of the king honours work and rates pay last.

Confucius

A good name is to be chosen rather than great riches.

The Bible

Money gives a man thirty years more of dignity.

Chinese proverb

One is not rich by what one owns, but more by what one is able to do without with dignity.

Immanuel Kant

Money is the only substance which can keep a cold world from nicknaming a citizen "Hey, you!"

Addison Mizner

Nothing but money counts nowadays: it wins honor, it wins friends; everywhere the poor man is down.

Ovid

Poverty of course is no disgrace, but it is damned annoying.

William Pitt

Distribution

The leaders of the French Revolution excited the poor against the rich; this made the rich poor, but it never made the poor rich.

Fisher Ames

There are two types among the rich: the haves and the have-mores.

Anonymous

What this country needs is not more money, but more people who have some of it.

Anonymous

Money is a commodity that is constantly changing hands—and people.

Anonymous

The dispute between Marx and the capitalist is merely concerned with the question who shall have money.

Emil Brunner

Unto whomsoever much is given, of him shall be much required.

The Bible

You don't make the poor richer by making the rich poorer.

Winston Churchill

Where large sums of money are concerned, it is advisable to trust nobody.

Agatha Christie

It is hard to be poor when there are so many rich fools at whose expense one could live.

Denis Diderot

As a general rule, nobody has money who ought to have it.

Benjamin Disraeli

Why shouldn't the American people take half my money from me? I took all of it from them.

Edward A. Filene

The ideal social state is not that in which each gets an equal amount of wealth, but in which each gets in proportion to his contribution to the general stock.

Henry George

I suffer no guilt complexes or conscience pangs about my wealth. The Lord may have been disproportionate, but that is how He—or nature, if you like—operates.

J. Paul Getty

The poor aren't any different from the rich—they just don't have as much money.

S. I. Hayakawa

God must love the rich or he wouldn't divide so much among so few of them.

H. L. Mencken

Society can transport money from rich to poor only in a leaky bucket.

Arthur M. Okun

Mr. Jones is wrong to suggest that I support the rich against the poor. To the Christian there is no class distinction—that idea was largely concocted by the working class.

Letter in the Reynold News
(England)

The rich, in particular, are necessarily interested to support that order of things which can alone secure them in the possession of their own advantages. Men of inferior wealth combine to defend those of superior wealth in the possession of their property, in order that men of superior wealth may combine to defend them in the possession of theirs.

Adam Smith

(Wealth is) a power usurped by the few, to compel the many to labor for their benefit.

Percy Bysshe Shelley

My master was yet wholly at a loss to understand what motives could incite this race of lawyers to perplex, disquiet, and weary themselves by engaging in a confederacy of injustice, merely for the sake of injuring their fellow-animals; neither could he comprehend what I meant in saying they did it for hire.

Jonathan Swift

America is an enormous frosted cupcake in the middle of millions of starving people.

Gloria Steinem

Wealth in modern societies is distributed according to opportunity; and while opportunity depends partly upon talent and energy, it depends still more upon birth, social position, access to education and inherited wealth; in a word, upon property.

R. H. Tawney

E

Ecology
Economy
Enjoyment
Envy
Evil, Evildoing
Excessiveness

Ecology

I am not quite sure what the advantage is in having a few more dollars to spend if the air is too dirty to breathe, the water too polluted to drink, the commuters are losing out in the struggle to get in and out of the city, the streets are filthy and the schools so bad that the young perhaps wisely stay away, and hoodlums roll citizens for some of the dollars they saved in the tax cut.

John Kenneth Galbraith

Economy

A study of economics usually reveals that the best time to buy anything is last year.

Marty Allen

Economy is a poor man's revenue; extravagance a rich man's ruin.

Anonymous

Economy: the wealth of the poor and the wisdom of the rich.

Alexandre Dumas (The Elder)

The petty economies of the rich are just as amazing as the silly extravagances of the poor.

William Feather

Economy is going without something you want, in case you should someday want something which you probably won't want.

Anthony Hope

The regard one shows economy, is like that we show an old aunt, who is to leave us something at last.

William Shenstone

Enjoyment

I'm so happy to be rich, I'm willing to take all the consequences.

Howard Ahmanson

In frolics dispose your pounds, shillings and pence;
For we shall be nothing a hundred years hence.

Anonymous

I'm tired of love, I'm still more tired of rhyme, but money gives me pleasure all the time.

Hilaire Belloc

It is no good making a fortune if you do not know how to enjoy it. Higher material standards are no good if you do not know how to use them for a better life. Economic ideals must include the ideal of beauty as well as the ideal of plenty. We want new capital, far more capital than is being created today, but we want it not only to advance material well-being but because we want a better and more beautiful life for the citizens.

Basil Blackett

If your capacity to acquire has outstripped your capacity to enjoy, you are on the way to the scrapheap.

Glen Buck

The best way to realize the pleasure of feeling rich is to live in a smaller house than your means would entitle you to have.

Edward Clarke

How pleasant it is to have money, heigh-ho!
How pleasant it is to have money!

Arthur Hugh Clough

(Wealth) Not his who has it, but his who enjoys it.

Benjamin Franklin

I believe you enjoy your wealth so much more since it was only after you longed for riches that you became wealthy.

Xenophon

The golden mean is that a man should strive in moderation to obtain wealth, in proportion to the wants of his household; and he should cheerfully enjoy that which his Creator has graciously bestowed upon him, for it is "the Lord's blessing which maketh rich."

Saadia Ben Joseph

Life is short. The sooner that a man begins to enjoy his wealth the better.

Samuel Johnson

Be rich to yourself and poor to your friends.

Juvenal

Do you know the only thing that gives me pleasure? It's to see my dividends coming in.

John D. Rockefeller

He enjoys riches most who needs them least.

Seneca

Economy, in the estimation of common minds, often means the absence of all taste and comfort.

Syden Smith

A heavy purse makes a light heart.

Irish proverb

Envy

Many speak the truth when they say that they despise riches, but they mean the riches possessed by other men.

Charles Caleb Colton

Let us not envy some men their accumulated riches; their burden would be too heavy for us; we could not sacrifice, as they do, health, quiet, honor and conscience, to obtain them: it is to pay so dear for them that the bargain is a loss.

Jean de La Bruyère

Those who condemn wealth are those who have none and see no chance of getting it.

William Penn Patrick

A tough lesson in life that one has to learn is that not everybody wishes you well.

Dan Rather

My little old man and I fell out.
I'll tell you what 'twas all about;
I had money and he had none,
And that's the way the row begun.

Nursery Rhyme

Probably the greatest harm done by vast wealth is the harm that we of moderate means do ourselves when we let the vices of envy and hatred enter deep into our own natures.

Theodore Roosevelt

Few of us can stand prosperity. Another man's, I mean.

Mark Twain

The people of this country are not jealous of fortunes, however great, which have been built up by the honest development of great enterprises, which have been actually earned by business energy and sagacity; they are jealous only of speculative wealth, of the wealth which has been piled up by no effort at all, but only by shrewd wits playing on the credulity of others. . . . This is "predatory wealth," and is found in stock markets.

Woodrow Wilson

The love of some one else's money is the root of all evil.

Anonymous

The best condition in life is not to be so rich as to be envied nor so poor as to be damned.

Josh Billings

Most of us hate to see a poor loser—or a rich winner.

Harold Coffin

Really, the ones who aren't amiable in life are the people who haven't got, not the ones who have. There's an awful lot of jealousy. People only resent wealth because they haven't got it. Why should one resent what other people have?

Mary Francis

He had a Puritan distaste for money in someone else's hand.

Roger Kahn

A man who shows me his wealth is like the beggar who shows me his poverty; they are both looking for alms, the rich man for the alms of my envy, the poor man for the alms of my guilt.

Ben Hecht

Evil, Evildoing

Money is not the root of all evil—no money is.

Anonymous

To the cynic, money isn't the root of all evil—evil is the root of all money.

Anonymous

The ways to enrich are many, and most of them foul.

Francis Bacon

A man seldom gets rich without ill-got gain; as a horse does not fatten without feeding in the night.

Chinese proverb

Money is the fruit of evil as often as the root.

Henry Fielding

When good befalls a man he calls it Providence, when evil Fate.

Knut Hamsun

The man who thinks that anything can be accomplished by money is likely to do anything for money.

Hebrew proverb

Wealth first, the ready pander of all sin,
Brought foreign manners, foreign vices in.

Juvenal

The lack of money is the root of all evil.

Mark Twain

Excessiveness

Minds like bodies, will often fall into a pimpled, ill-conditioned state from mere excess of comfort.

Charles Dickens

A billion dollars here, a billion dollars there, and pretty soon you're talking about real money.

Everett Dirksen

It's possible to own too much. A man with one watch knows what time it is; a man with two watches is never quite sure.

Lee Segall

To have enough is good luck, to have more than enough is harmful. This is true of all things, but especially of money.

Chuang-Tzu

A man is never so on trial as in the moment of excessive good fortune.

Lew Wallace

F

Family
Freedom
Friendship
Frugality

Family

A millionaire is the only person who receives letters from second cousins.

Anonymous

By the time a family pays off the mortgage for a home in the suburbs, the home isn't home, and the suburbs aren't suburbs.

Anonymous

There are several ways in which to apportion the family income, all of them unsatisfactory.

Robert Benchley

Only the rich have distant relatives.

Chinese proverb

A father is a banker provided by nature.

French proverb

Poor relatives are distant relatives.

Hebrew proverb

Money without children is riches without savor.

Hebrew proverb

A married man with a family will do anything for money.

Charles de Talleyrand

The richer a relative is, the less he bothers you.

Kin Hubbard

A poor relation is the most irrelevant thing in nature.

Charles Lamb

(Wealth is a) good wife and health.

Charles Haddon Spurgeon

Freedom

(Money) The symbol of everything that is necessary for man's well-being and happiness . . . Money means freedom, independence, liberty.

Edward E. Beals

To rail at money, to wax indignant against it, is silly. Money is nothing; its power is purely symbolical. Money is the sign of liberty. To curse money is to curse liberty—to curse life, which is nothing, if it be not free.

Rémy de Gourmont

If a nation values anything more than freedom, it will lose its freedom; and the irony of it is that if it is comfort or money that it values more, it will lose that too.

William Sommerset Maugham

If we command our wealth, we shall be rich and free; if our wealth commands us, we are poor indeed.

Edmund Burke

With his own money a person can live as he likes—a ruble that's your own is dearer than a brother.

Maxim Gorky

You cannot decree women to be sexually free when they are not economically free.

Shere Hite

Lives based on having are less free than lives based either on doing or on being.

William James

(Money is) health, and liberty, and strength.

Charles Lamb

The seven deadly sins . . . Food, clothing, firing, rent, taxes, respectability and children. Nothing can lift those seven millstones from man's neck but money: and the spirit cannot soar until the millstones are lifted.

George Bernard Shaw

Wealth I ask not, hope nor love,
Nor a friend to know me;
All I ask, the heavens above,
And the road below me.

Robert Louis Stevenson

A man is rich in proportion to the things he can afford to let alone.

Thoreau

Friendship

Some people may have their first dollar, but the man who is really rich is the one who still has his first friend.

Anonymous

The holy passion of friendship is of so sweet and steady and loyal and enduring a nature that it will last through a whole lifetime, if not asked to lend money.

Mark Twain

In prosperity friends do not leave you unless desired, whereas in adversity they stay away of their own accord.

Demetrius

A full wallet is the best companion.

Anonymous

Friendship is like money, easier made than kept.

Samuel Butler

In prosperity our friends know us; in adversity we know our friends.

Churton Collins

No one is rich enough to do without a neighbor.

Danish proverb

Business, you know, may bring money, but friendship hardly ever does.

Jane Austen

There are three faithful friends: an old wife, an old dog, and ready money.

Bejamin Franklin

Money makes not so many true friends as real enemies.

Thomas Fuller

Help me to money and I'll help myself to friends.

Thomas Fuller

Better the friend we can see than the money we cannot!

Greek proverb

It is better in times of need to have a friend rather than money.

Greek proverb

A man's standing with his friends depends on his financial position.

Plautus

The happiest miser on earth is the man who saves up every friend he can make.

Robert E. Sherwood

Frugality

Frugality means the contrary of extravagance. It does not mean stinginess; it does not mean pinching; but it means an abstaining from all unnecessary expenditure and all unnecessary use of goods of any and of every sort. It is a quality of great importance, whether the rank in life be high or low.

William A. Alcott

Frugality is the sure guardian of our virtues.

Braham proverb

Frugality includes all the other virtues.

Cicero

Industry must make a purse, and frugality finds strings for it.

Esther Copley

Frugality is misery in disguise.

Publilius

If frugality were established in the state, if our expenses were laid out rather in the necessaries than the superfluities of life, there might be fewer wants, and even fewer pleasures, but infinitely more happiness.

Oliver Goldsmith

Righteousness, or justice, is, undoubtedly of all the virtues, the surest foundation on which to create and establish a new state. But there are two nobler virtues, industry and frugality, which tend more to increase the wealth, power and grandeur of the community, than all the others without them.

Benjamin Franklin

Remember, that time is money. . . . Remember, that credit is money. . . . Remember, that money is of the prolific, generating nature. . . . Remember, that six pounds a year is but a groat a day. . . . Remember this saying, The good payer is lord of another man's purse, He that is known to pay punctually and exactly to the time he promises, may at any time, and on any occasion, raise all the money his friends can spare. . . . In short, the way to wealth, if you desire it, is as plain as the way to market. It depends chiefly on two words, industry and frugality; that is, waste neither time nor money, but make the best use of both.

Benjamin Franklin

Frugality is an enriching virtue: a virtue I never could acquire myself; but I was lucky to find it in a wife, who thereby became a fortune to me. With frugality, there will be no lack; with extravagance, there's never enough.

Benjamin Franklin

With parsimony a little is sufficient; without it nothing is sufficient; but frugality makes a poor man rich.

Seneca

G

Gambling
Generosity
Gold
Government
Gratification

Gambling

The urge to gamble is so universal and its practice so pleasurable that I assume it must be evil.

Heywood Broun

The darkest hour of any man's life is when he sits down to plan how to get money without earning it.

Horace Greeley

The only man who makes money following the races is the one who does so with a broom and shovel.

Elbert Hubbard

The safest way to double your money is to fold it over once and put it in your pocket.

Kin Hubbard

Anybody who finds it easy to make money on the horses is probably in the dog-food business.

Franklin P. Jones

The best throw of the dice is to throw them away.

Austin O'Malley

Generosity

Do you remember the generosity of Jesus Christ, the Lord of us all? He was rich beyond our telling, yet he became poor for your sakes so that his poverty might make you rich.

The Bible

And he looked up, and saw the rich men casting their gifts into the treasury. And he saw also a certain poor widow casting in thither two mites. And he said, Of a truth I say unto you, that this poor widow hath cast in more than they all: For all these have of their abundance cast in unto the offerings of God: but she of her penury hath cast in all the living that she had.

The Bible

I was ahungered, and ye gave me meat; I was thirsty, and ye gave me drink: I was a stranger, and ye took me in.

The Bible

Money was made for the free-hearted and generous.

John Gay

Poverty robs one of the right to be generous.

George Gissing

I do not know how wicked American millionaires are, but as I travel about and see the results of their generosity in the form of hospitals, churches, public libraries, universities, parks, recreation grounds, art museums and theatres I wonder what on earth we should do without them.

William Lyon Phelps

The poor are the only consistent altruists; they sell all that they have and give to the rich.

Holbrook Jackson

We'd all like a reputation for generosity and we'd all like to buy it cheap.

Mignon McLaughlin

Generous people are rarely mentally ill people.

Karl Menninger

I would have a man generous to his country, his neighbors, his kindred, his friends, and most of all his poor friends. Not like some who are most lavish with those who are able to give most to them.

Pliny

I owe much; I have nothing; the rest I leave to the poor.

François Rabelais

Let the man who has and doesn't give
Break his neck, and cease to live!
Let him who gives without a care
Gather rubies from the air.

James Stephens

Gold

The possession of gold has ruined fewer men than the lack of it.

Thomas Bailey Aldrich

(Gold is) a metal men dig out of holes for dentists and governments to put back in.

Anonymous

If all the gold in the world were melted down into a solid cube it would be about the size of an eight-room house. If a man got possession of all that gold—billions of dollars worth, he could not buy a friend, character, peace of mind, clear conscience, or a sense of eternity.

Charles F. Banning

(Gold is) a deep-persuading orator.

Richard Barnfield

Gold loves to make its way through the midst of sentinels and to break through rocks, for it is mightier than the thunderbolt.

Horace

Gold lends a touch of beauty even to the ugly.

Nicolas Boileau

The golden age only comes to men when they have forgotten gold.

G. K. Chesterton

Gold does friendship separate;
Gold does civil wars create.

Abraham Cowley

(Gold is) a transient, shining trouble.

James Grainger

Gold! Gold! Gold! Gold!
Good or bad a thousand-fold!
How widely its agencies vary—
To save—to ruin—to curse—to bless—
As even its minted coins express,
Now stamp'd with the image of Good Queen Bess,
And now of a Bloody Mary.

Thomas Hood

Building one's life on a foundation of gold is just like building a house on foundations of sand.

Henrik Ibsen

The lust of gold, unfeeling and remorseless,
The last corruption of degenerate man.

Samuel Johnson

It is extraordinary how many emotional storms one may weather in safety if one is ballasted with ever so little gold.

William McFee

Gold is the key, whatever else we try;
And that sweet metal aids the conqueror
in every case, in love as well as war.

Molière

He who loves gold is a fool; he who fears it, is a slave; he who adores it, an idolator; he who hoards it up, a dunce; he who uses it, is the wise man.

Old Farmer's Almanac

Gold will buy the highest honours; and gold will purchase love.

Ovid

(Gold is) a living god.

Percy Bysshe Shelley

My heart does not hanker after gold, no matter how desirable, nor do I thirst to drink from a jewelled flask.

Propertius

Gold is the blood of society. Too little or too much is unhealthy for its possessor.

Hasidic saying

The chains of love are never so binding as when the links are made of gold.

Royal Tyler

Gold is the spirit of society.

Paul Valéry

Government

I sometimes feel bad about how much I take as a teenager but we do get ripped off by the government. Jeez, someday I've got to do something about that.

Linda Blair

It is to be regretted that the rich and powerful too often bend the acts of government to their selfish purposes.

Andrew Jackson

When one may pay out over two million dollars to presidential and Congressional campaigns, the U.S. Government is virtually up for sale.

John Gardner

Money, and nor mortality, is the principle of commercial nations.

Thomas Jefferson

The hopes of the Republic cannot forever tolerate either undeserved poverty or self-serving wealth.

Franklin Delano Roosevelt

In general, the art of the government consists of taking as much money as possible from one class of citizens to give to the other.

Voltaire

Gratification

Money is sweet balm.

Arab proverb

Riches increase to a monstrous extent; yet there is always something wanting to our still imperfect fortune.

Horace

It's not really worth much—being rich—too much money seems to take the taste and colour out of things. It oughtn't to do, but it does, damn it.

J. B. Priestley

(Riches are) larger means to gratify the will.

William Congreve

Nothing but money is sweeter than honey.

Benjamin Franklin

The suffering of the rich is among the sweetest pleasures of the poor.

R. M. Huber

I don't want to make money. I just want to be wonderful.

Marilyn Monroe

How sweetly one guinea rhymes to another and how they dance to the music of their own clink.

William Congreve

H

Happiness
Health
Hoarding
Honesty

Happiness

Pronounce no man happy before his death, for by his latter end he shall a man be known.

Apocrypha

The bird of paradise alights only upon the hand that does not grasp.

John Berry

Where your treasure is, there will your heart be also.

The Bible

The happiest time in any man's life is when he is in red-hot pursuit of a dollar with a reasonable prospect of overtaking it.

Josh Billings

Money will buy a pretty good dog but it won't buy the wag of his tail.

Josh Billings

Money doesn't always bring happiness. People with ten million dollars are no happier than people with nine million dollars.

Hobart Brown

It is impossible for man's happiness to consist in wealth. For wealth is two-fold . . . natural and artificial. Natural wealth is that which serves man as a remedy for his natural wants, such as food, drink, clothing, conveyances, dwellings, and things of this kind, while artificial wealth is that which is not a direct help to nature, as money, but is invented by the art of man for the convenience of exchange and as a measure of things saleable.

Now it is evident that man's happiness cannot consist in natural wealth. For wealth of this kind is sought as a support of human nature; consequently it cannot be man's last end, but rather is ordered to man as to its end. Therefore in the order of nature, all such things are below man, and made for him. . . .

And as to artificial wealth, it is not sought save for the sake of natural wealth, since man would not seek it except that by its means he procures for himself the necessaries of life. Consequently much less does it have the character of the last end. Therefore it is impossible for happiness, which is the last end of man, to consist in wealth.

Saint Thomas Aquinas

What is the worth of anything
But for the happiness 'twill bring?

R. O. Cambridge

The object of living is work, experience, happiness. There is joy in work. All that money can do is buy us some one else's work in exchange for our own. There is no happiness except in the realization that we have accomplished something.

Henry Ford

True happiness flows from the possession of wisdom and virtue and not from the possession of external goods.

Aristotle

Happiness seems to require a modicum of external prosperity.

Aristotle

A large income is the best recipe for happiness I ever heard of. It certainly may secure all the myrtle and turkey part of it.

Jane Austen

It's a kind of spiritual snobbery that makes people think they can be happy without money.

Albert Camus

Not to be avaricious is money; not to be fond of buying is a revenue; but to be content with our own is the greatest and most certain wealth of all.

Cicero

May we never let the things we can't have, or don't have, or shouldn't have, spoil our enjoyment of the things we do have and can have. As we value our happiness let us not forget it, for one of the greatest lessons in life is learning to be happy without the things we cannot or should not have.

Richard L. Evans

There are two ways of being happy: We must either diminish our wants or augment our means—either may do—the result is the same and it is for each man to decide for himself and to do that which happens to be easier.

Benjamin Franklin

Money never made a man happy yet, nor will it. There is nothing in its nature to produce happiness. The more a man has, the more he wants. That was a true proverb of the wise man, rely upon it: "Better is little with the fear of the Lord, than great treasure, and trouble therewith."

Benjamin Franklin

(Money is) a merry fellow.

Thomas Fuller

I wondered why anyone so rich and so beautiful should ever be unhappy—for I had been schooled by poverty to believe that money is the first essential of happiness—and yet her unhappiness was as evident as her beauty, or the luxury that enveloped her.

Ellen Glasgow

Alas! the joys that fortune brings
Are trifling and decay;
And those who prize the paltry things,
More trifling still than they.

Oliver Goldsmith

. . . a poor person who is unhappy is in a better position than a rich person who is unhappy. Because the poor person has hope. He thinks money would help.

Jean Kerr

How can true happiness proceed from wealth, which in its acquisition causes pain; in loss, affliction; in abundance, folly.

Hitopadesa

The house laughs with silver.

Horace

It's pretty hard to tell what brings happiness; poverty and wealth have both failed.

Kin Hubbard

If I owe Smith ten dollars, and God forgives me, that doesn't pay Smith.

Robert Green Ingersoll

Riches enoble a man's circumstances, but not himself.

Immanuel Kant

One says that money doesn't make happiness. Without doubt one was speaking of the money of others.

Sacha Guitry

Great wealth cannot still hunger, but rather occasions more dearth; for where rich people are, there things are always dear. Moreover, money makes no man merry, but much rather pensive and full of sorrow.

Martin Luther

Happiness lies in taste and not in material things.

La Rochefoucauld

We were happier when we were poorer, but we were also younger.

Charles Lamb

If I were honest, I would admit that money is one half of happiness; it makes it so much more attractive!

Marie Leneru

Humanly speaking, it is only when the hair is white, when . . . life is almost over, that men begin to realize how hopelessly elusive is the happiness promised by wealth and fame.

Joseph McSorley

Riches cover a multitude of woes.

Menander

I have no money, no resources, no hopes. I am the happiest man alive.

Henry Miller

I believe the recipe for happiness to be just enough money to pay the monthly bills and acquire a little surplus to give you confidence, a little too much work each day, enthusiasm for your work, a substantial share of good health, a couple of real friends, and a wife and children to share life's beauty with you.

J. Kenfield Morley

If you are content, you have enough to live comfortably.

Plautus

False happiness is like false money; it passes for a time as well as the true, and serves some ordinary occasions; but when it is brought to the touch, we find the lightness and alloy, and feel the loss.

Alexander Pope

(Wealth is) a contented mind.

Mohammed

We have produced a world of contented bodies and discontented minds.

Adam Clayton Powell

It is wrong to assume that men of immense wealth are always happy.

John D. Rockefeller, Sr.

Wealth must justify itself in happiness.

George Santayana

What riches have you that you deem me poor,
Or what large comfort that you call me sad?
Tell me what makes you so exceeding glad:
Is your earth happy or your heaven sure?

George Santayana

Money is human happiness in the abstract: he, then, who is no longer capable of enjoying human happiness in the concrete devotes himself utterly to money.

Schopenhauer

. . . Some day people will learn that material things do not bring happiness, and are of little use in making people creative and powerful . . .

Charles P. Steinmetz

He that wants money, means, and content is without three good friends.

Shakespeare

I thank God, who has made me poor, that He has made me merry.

Sydney Smith

Of no mortal say "That man is happy," till vexed by no grievous ill he pass Life's goal.

Sophocles

If there are people at once rich and content, be assured that they are content because they know how to be so, not because they are rich.

Charles Wagner

Money makes a man laugh.

John Selden

(Money is) an article which may be used as a Universal passport to everywhere except heaven, and as a universal provider of everything except happiness.

Wall Street Journal

There's no more happiness with ten servants than with one.

Marylou Whitney

Health

If medical science continues to prolong human life, some of us may eventually pay off the mortgage.

Anonymous

We should manage our fortune as we do our health—enjoy it when good, be patient when it is bad, and never apply violent remedies except in an extreme necessity.

La Rochefoucauld

O health! health! the blessing of the rich! the riches of the poor! who can buy thee at too dear a rate, since there is no enjoying this world without thee?

Ben Jonson

He who has health, has hope; and he who has hope, has everything.

Arabian proverb

(The dollar is) a piece of green paper having healing properties.

Jerry Dashkin

More wealth, less health.

French proverb

There's another advantage of being poor—a doctor will cure you faster.

Kin Hubbard

The man with a million is seldom as happy as the man who feels like a million.

Anonymous

The only way for a rich man to be healthy is by exercise and abstinence to live as if he were poor.

William Temple

If you are going to have doctors you had better have doctors well off; just as if you are going to have a landlord you had better have a rich landlord. Taking all the round of professions and occupations, you will find that every man is the worse for being poor; and the doctor is a specially dangerous man when poor.

George Bernard Shaw

Look to your health; and if you have it, praise God, and value it next to a good conscience; for health is the second blessing that we mortals are capable of; a blessing that money cannot buy.

Ezaak Walton

Hoarding

I will say to myself, "Man, you have plenty of good things laid by, enough for many years: take life easy, eat, drink, and enjoy yourself." But God said to him, "You fool, this very night you must surrender your life; you have made your money—who will get it now?"

The Bible

It is not a crime to be rich, nor a virtue to be poor . . . The sin lies in hoarding wealth and keeping it from circulating freely to all who need it.

Charles Fillmore

The amassing of wealth is one of the worst species of idolatry, no idol more debasing.

Andrew Carnegie

What good does this huge weight of gold and silver, if fear forces you to bury it secretly in the ground?

Horace

Riches are intended for the comfort of life, and not life for the purpose of hoarding riches.

Sa'Di

To a hoarding father succeeds an extravagant son.

Spanish proverb

Honesty

'Tis my opinion every man cheats in his way, and he is only honest who is not discovered.

Susannah Centlivre

Every man should make up his mind that if he expects to succeed, he must give an honest return for the other man's dollar.

E. H. Harriman

[In the Essenes' Manual of Discipline] any man who lied regarding money would be excluded from the Banquet of the Many and could receive only one-fourth of his food for the next year.

Janet Barkas

No one can earn a million dollars honestly.

William Jennings Bryan

Honesty is as rare as a man without self-pity.

Stephen Vincent Benet

He that resolves to deal with none but honest men, must leave off dealing.

Thomas Fuller

Honesty—after the first million!

Horace

Let none of us delude himself by supposing that honesty is always the best policy. It is not.

Dean Inge

I have not observed men's honesty to increase with their riches.

Thomas Jefferson

A show of a certain amount of honesty is in any profession or business the surest way of growing rich.

Jean de La Bruyère

There is one way to find out if a man is honest—ask him. If he says 'yes,' you know he is crooked.

Groucho Marx

If honesty did not exist, we ought to invent it as the best means of getting rich.

Horace Mirabeau

Honesty is for the most part less profitable than dishonesty.

Plato

Honesty is the best policy—when there is money in it.

Mark Twain

I

Importance
Indebtedness
Independence
Inflation
Inheritance
Initiative
Inspiration
Intelligence
Investment

Importance

Money buys everything except love, personality, freedom, immortality.

Anonymous

Money may not buy everything, but it's a great consolation until you have everything.

Anonymous

Money isn't everything, but it's way ahead of any of its competitors.

Anonymous

Regardless of finance, inflation or taxation, the real problem always turns out to be money.

Anonymous

She is the sovereign queen of all delights;
For her the lawyer pleads, the soldier fights.

Richard Barnfield

(Wealth is) not an end of life, but an instrument of life.

Henry Ward Beecher

Money wasn't that important. Money doesn't help you sleep. Money doesn't help your mother be well, money doesn't make your brother stay interested in his studies, money doesn't help an argument when nobody knows what they're arguing about. Money doesn't help nothing. Money is only good when you've got something else to do with it. A man can lose everything, family, all your dreams, and still have a pocketful of money.

George Foreman

Money is a defense.

The Bible

(Money is) the best foundation in the world.

Miguel de Cervantes

Many priceless things can be bought.

Maria Von Ebner-Eschenbach

One is weary of hearing about the omnipotence of money. I will say rather that, for a genuine man, it is no evil to be poor.

Thomas Carlyle

When I think of all the sorrow and the barrenness that has been wrought in my life by want of a few more pounds per annum than I was able to earn, I stand aghast at money's significance.

George Gissing

I haven't any time to make money, and I don't want any anyhow. Money is more trouble than it's worth.

Horace Greeley

Money. The root of all good.

Minnesota Fats

Money can buy anything—except sense.

Hebrew proverb

The world rests on three things: Money, money, and money.

Hebrew proverb

Money is life to us wretched mortals.

Hesiod

High descent and meritorious deeds, unless united to wealth, are as useless as sea-weed.

Horace

Some folks get credit for having horse sense that hain't ever had enough money to make fools of themselves.

Kin Hubbard

(Money is) another kind of blood.

Latin proverb

Wealth is the smallest thing on earth, the least gift that God has bestowed on mankind.

Martin Luther

(Money is) the best advocate.

Mendele

The dollars aren't important—once you have them.

Johnny Miller

Leave off the agony, leave off the style,
Unless you've got money by you all the while.

Julia A. Moore

Certainly, there are lots of things in life that money won't buy, but it's very funny—have you ever tried to buy them without money?

Ogden Nash

. . . It represents health, strength, honour, generosity and beauty . . . Not the least of its virtues is that it destroys base people as certainly as it fortifies and dignifies noble people.

George Bernard Shaw

And Wealth, more bright with Virtue joined,
Brings golden Opportunity.

Pindar

Always bring money along with your complaints.

Plautus

(Money is) a good soldier.

Shakespeare

If money go before, all ways do lie open.

Shakespeare

Money is the counter that enables life to be lived socially: it is life as truly as sovereigns and banknotes are money.

George Bernard Shaw

(Money is) the most important thing in the world.

George Bernard Shaw

When I was young I thought that money was the most important thing in life; now that I am old I know that it is.

Oscar Wilde

Let all the learned say what they can,
'Tis ready money makes the man.

William Somerville

Nothing that is God's is obtainable by money.

Tertullian

Money—money, like everything else—is a deception and a disappointment.

H. G. Wells

There are few sorrows, however poignant, in which a good income is of no avail.

Logan P. Smith

Indebtedness

The only way some people can get out of debt is by refinancing the mortgage on their house.

Anonymous

It is better to pay a creditor than to give to a friend.

Aristotle

All progress is based upon the universal innate desire on the part of every organism to live beyond its income.

Samuel Butler

Some men are known by their deeds, others by their mortgages.

Anonymous

There's plenty of money around; the trouble is, everyone owes it to everyone else.

Anonymous

(Money is) a device which permits people to get into debt a little further.

Anonymous

What with time payments, charge accounts and credit cards, about all you can do with money nowadays is to owe it.

Anonymous

If it isn't the sheriff, it's the finance company; I've got more attachments on me than a vacuum cleaner.

John Barrymore

Annual income twenty pounds, annual expenditure nineteen ninety-six, result happiness. Annual income twenty pounds, annual expenditure twenty pounds ought and six, result misery.

Charles Dickens

Always pay; for first and last you must pay your entire debt.

Ralph Waldo Emerson

(Wealth is) owing nothing.

Hungarian proverb

Do not accustom yourself to consider debt only as an inconvenience. You will find it a calamity.

Samuel Johnson

In the midst of life we are in debt.

Ethel Watts Mumford

Debt is the secret foe of thrift, as vice and idleness are its open foes. The debt-habit is the twin brother of poverty.

T.T. Munger

Some people use one-half their ingenuity to get into debt, and the other half to avoid paying it.

George D. Prentice

The first step in debt is like the first step in falsehood, involving the necessity of going on in the same course, debt following debt, as lie follows lie.

S. Smiles

One of the swiftest toboggans I know of is for a young man to get into debt.

John D. Rockefeller

Tears pay no debts.

Talmud

If you think nobody cares if you're alive, try missing a couple of car payments.

Earl Wilson

Independence

To be poor and independent is very nearly an impossibility.

William Cobbett

If money is your hope for independence you will never have it. The only real security that a man can have in this world is a reserve of knowledge, experience and ability.

Henry Ford

It's easy to be independent when you've got money. But to be independent when you haven't got a thing—that's the Lord's test.

Mahalia Jackson

Let all your views in life be directed to a solid, however moderate, independence; without it no man can be happy, nor even honest.

Junius

Inflation

What this country needs is a good five-cent nickel.

Franklin Pierce Adams

Money doesn't go very far these days, or come very near.

Anonymous

A $10 million windfall? At today's prices, I'd feel almost as rich as I did one day in 1936 when I found a dime on the sidewalk and blew the whole wad on 20 Mary Jane candy bars, a box of jujubes and a double feature.

Russell Baker

No one will deny the importance of urging rich and poor alike, in the present state of things to try and economise the fuel and food which they may have at their disposal. The sooner we make up our minds that what we regretfully speak of as the "good old days" with their good old prices, will never come again, the sooner we shall cease to look fondly back on a cheaper past, and brace ourselves helpfully and bravely to face the increased cost of the necessaries of life.

Lady Barker

Inflation is the most important fact of our time, the single greatest peril of our economic health.

Bernard M. Baruch

(Inflation means) being broke with a lot of money in your pocket.

Pauli Brussell

Having a little inflation is like being a little pregnant—inflation feeds on itself and quickly passes the "little" mark.

Diana Cohen

The cost of living has gone up another dollar a quart.

W.C. Fields

Inflation is the one form of taxation that can be imposed without legislation.

Milton Friedman

Inflation is defined as the quality that makes balloons larger and candy bars smaller.

General Features Corporation

(Inflation is) when you never had it so good or parted with it so fast.

Max Hess

One of the benefits of inflation is that kids can no longer get sick on a nickel's worth of candy.

Journeyman Barber Magazine

Inflation is bringing us true democracy. For the first time in history, luxuries and necessities are selling at the same price.

Robert Orben

(Inflation is) the world's most successful thief.

Carl E. Person

A dollar may not go as far as it once did, but it makes up for it in speed.

Ned Preston

The uprisings of 1789 cost Louis XVI some prerogatives, but four years later a valueless currency cost him his head. Germany's inflation of the 1920's laid the foundation upon which Hitler built. Indeed, a runaway inflation is the goal of revolutionists. The maxim of that apostle of revolution, Lenin, was "Debauch the currency!"

Edgar M. Queeny

A dollar saved today is seventy-five cents earned tomorrow.

James Reston

Invest in inflation. It's the only thing going up.

Will Rogers

Inheritance

People don't have fortunes left them . . . nowadays; men have to work, and women to marry for money. It's a dreadfully unjust world. . . .

Louisa May Alcott

A millionaire is a man who gathers a fortune he doesn't need to leave to people who don't deserve it.

Anonymous

I believe in inherited wealth. Society needs to have some people who are above it all.

Edward Digby Baltzell, Jr.

When you have told anyone you have left him a legacy, the only decent thing to do is to die at once.

Samuel Butler

"Yet doth he live," exclaims the impatient heir,
And sighs for sables that he may not wear.

George Gordon Byron

Gentility is what is left over from rich ancestors after the money is gone.

John Ciardi

All heiresses are beautiful.

John Dryden

When a man's wealth diminishes, even his children don't accept his opinion.

Ibn Gabirol

Hereditary wealth is in reality a premium paid to idleness.

William Godwin

The way to make thy son rich is to fill
His mind with rest, before his trunk with riches;
For wealth without contentment climbs a hill
To feel those tempests which fly over ditches.

George Herbert

There is nothing earthly that lasts so well, on the whole, as money. A man's learning dies with him; even his virtues fade out of remembrance; but the dividends on the stocks he bequeaths to his children live and keep his memory green.

Oliver Wendell Holmes

If a man dies and leaves his estate in an uncertain condition, the lawyers become his heirs.

Ed Howe

There is inherited wealth in this country and also inherited poverty.

John F. Kennedy

The rich man's sons inherits cares;
The bank may break, the factory burn,
A breath may burst his bubble shares,
And soft white hands could hardly earn
A living that would serve his turn.

James Russell Lowell

A son can bear with composure the death of his father, but the loss of his inheritance might drive him to despair.

Machiavelli

It is not easy to find the relatives of a poor man.

Menander

Inherited wealth is a big handicap to happiness. It is as certain death to ambition as cocaine is to morality.

W. K. Vanderbilt

Initiative

If you want to get rich, you son of a bitch,
I'll tell you what to do:
Never sit down with a tear or a frown,
And paddle your own canoe.

Anonymous

Let a man start out in life to build something better and sell it cheaper than it has been built or sold before, let him have that determination and the money will roll in.

Henry Ford

To think twice in every matter and follow the lead of others is no way to make money.

Ihara Saikaku

Inspiration

To force myself to earn more money, I determined to spend more.

James Agate

Money never starts an idea; it is the idea that starts the money.

W. J. Cameron

Hold your thoughts on . . . money by concentration, or fixation of attention, with your eyes closed, until you can actually see the physical appearance of money. Do this at least once a day.

Napoleon Hill

That some should be rich, shows that others may become rich, and hence is just encouragement to industry and enterprize.

Abraham Lincoln

Intelligence

The fool and the brutish person perish, and leave their wealth to others.

The Bible

Do not be fooled into believing that because a man is rich he is necessarily smart. There is ample proof to the contrary.

Julius Rosenwald

If these distracted times prove anything, they prove that the greatest illusion is reliance upon the security and permanence of material possessions. We must search for some other coin. And we will discover that the treasure-house of education has stood intact and unshaken in the storm. The man of cultivated life has founded his house upon a rock. You can never take away the magnificent mansion of his mind.

John Cudahy

Now that he was rich he was not thought ignorant any more, but simply eccentric.

Mavis Gallant

He that hath money in his purse cannot want a head for his shoulders.

James Howell

There are two very bad things in this American land of ours, the worship of money and the worship of intellect. Both money and intellect are regarded as good in themselves, and you consequently see the possessor of either eager to display his possessions to the public, and win the public recognition of the fact. But intellect is as essentially subordinate a good as money is. It is good only as a minister and purveyor to right affections.

Henry James, Sr.

To be clever enough to get a great deal of money, one must be stupid enough to want it.

G.K. Chesterton

A purely materialistic philosophy is to me the height of unintelligence.

Robert A. Millikan

(Wealth) A pretty promotor of intelligence, since it multiplies the avenues for its reception.

Donald G. Mitchell

Wealth is the product of man's capacity to think.

Ayn Rand

Investment

Old men are always advising young men to save money. That is bad advice. Don't save every nickel. Invest in yourself. I never saved a dollar until I was 40 years old.

Henry Ford

If a man empties his purse into his head, no one can take it away from him. An investment in knowledge always pays the best interest.

Benjamin Franklin

It is very much easier for a rich man to invest and grow richer than for the poor man to begin investing at all. And this is also true of nations.

Barbara Ward

Don't gamble! Take all your savings and buy some good stock and hold it 'til it goes up, then sell it. If it don't go up, don't buy it.

Will Rogers

Put not your trust in money. Put your money in trust.

Oliver Wendell Holmes

The best investment on earth is earth.

Louis Glickman

Never invest your money in anything that eats or needs repairing.

Billy Rose

Character and personal force are the only investments that are worth anything.

Walt Whitman

K

Knowledge

Knowledge

Knowledge cannot be stolen from us. It cannot be bought or sold. We may be poor, and the sheriff may come and sell our furniture, or drive away our cow, or take our pet lamb, and leave us homeless and penniless; but he cannot lay the law's hand upon the jewelry of the minds.

Burritt

They say that knowledge is power. I used to think so, but I now know that they meant money . . . Every guinea is a philosopher's stone . . . Cash is virtue.

George Gordon Byron

It is idle talking to a scholar in search of truth who is ashamed of poor clothes and poor food.

Confucius

(Money) enables a man to get along without an education, and education enables him to get along without money.

Marcelene Cox

What I know about money, I learned the hard way—by having had it.

Margaret Halsey

L

Labor

Law

Legitimacy

Leisure

Lending

Loss

Love

Love of Money

Luck

Labor

Money is all that is worth all your labors; Crowd your competitors, nix on your neighbors.

Franklin Pierce Adams

Labor (is) one of the processes by which A acquires the property for B.

Ambrose Bierce

My agent gets ten percent of everything I get, except my blinding headaches.

Fred Allen

It is not the employer who pays wages—he only handles the money. It is the product that pays wages.

Henry Ford

We are not the bosses of taxpayers; they are ours.

T. Coleman Andrews
(Tax Collector)

Be the business never so painful, you may have it done for the money.

Thomas Fuller

Wealth is a power usurped by the few to compel the many to labor for their benefit.

Percy Bysshe Shelley

The most popular labor-saving device is still money.

Phyllis George

A man is seldom so harmlessly occupied as when he is making money.

Samuel Johnson

Law

The real fight today is against inhuman, relentless exercise of capitalistic power . . . The present struggle in which we are engaged is for social and industrial justice.

Louis D. Brandeis

A gentleman considers what is right; the vulgar consider what will pay.

Confucius

Laws grind the poor, and rich men rule the law.

Oliver Goldsmith

When there's a rift in the lute, the business of the lawyer is to widen the rift and gather the loot.

Arthur Garfield Hays

There are only two classes in society: those who get more than they earn, and those who earn more than they get.

Holbrook Johnson

There is no contract you can't get out of for money.

Newton Minow

When there's a will, there's a lawsuit.

Addison Mizner

Legitimacy

Money makes everything legitimate, even bastards.

Hebrew proverb

(A wealthy person is) a scoundrel or the heir of one.

Spanish proverb

Leisure

If wealth is to be valued because it gives leisure, clearly it would be a mistake to sacrifice leisure in the struggle for wealth.

John Lubbock

The life of the rich is one long Sunday.

Georg Buchner

Of hobbies there are many, many, kinds. For example, money-making. But money-making is not exactly a hobby, for it will scarcely carry a boy along in continuous joy, comfort and pleasure—to say nothing of a full-grown man. Money comes, not because it is ridden as a hobby, but because a real hobby is ridden so cleverly and carefully that it oozes out money on the side!

John Cotton Dana

Much work is merely a way to make money;
Much leisure is merely a way to spend it.

C. Wright Mills

I would not exchange my leisure hours for all the wealth in the world.

Comte de Mirabeau

The thing that I should wish to obtain from money would be leisure with security.

Bertrand Russell

Lending

A moneylender serves you in the present tense, lends you in the conditional mood, keeps you in the subjunctive, and ruins you in the future.

Joseph Addison

I do not regard a broker as a member of the human race.

Honoré de Balzac

The borrower is servant to the lender.

The Bible

Whatever you lend let it be your money, and not your name. Money you may get again, and, if not, you may contrive to do without it; name once lost you cannot get again, and, if you cannot contrive to do without it, you had better never have been born.

Henry Bulwer

It is better to give than to lend, but it costs about the same.

Philip Gibbs

Plenty and indigence depend upon the opinion every one has of them; and riches, like glory or health, have no more beauty or pleasure than their possessor is pleased to lend them.

Michel de Montaigne

Never loan shylock money to a woman because you can't beat her up to collect.

Mafia motto

The man who won't loan money isn't going to have many friends—or need them.

Addison Mizner

A banker is a person who is willing to make a loan if you present sufficient evidence to show you don't need it.

Herbert V. Prochnow

Borrowers are nearly always ill spenders, and it is with lent money that all evil is mainly done and all unjust war protracted.

John Ruskin

Neither a borrower nor a lender be:
For loan oft loses both itself and a friend,
And borrowing dulls the edge of husbandry.

Shakespeare

The person whom you favoured with a loan, if he be a good man, will think himself in your debt after he has paid you.
Richard Steele

You can't force anyone to love you or to lend you money.
Jewish proverb

Loss

The trouble is not that you cannot take it with you, but that you cannot even keep it while you're here.
Anonymous

Bankruptcy is a legal preceeding in which you put your money in your pants pocket and give your coat to your creditors.
Joey Adams

He that resteth upon gains certain, shall hardly grow to great riches: and he that puts all upon adventures, doth oftentimes break and come to poverty: it is good therefore to guard adventures with certainties that may uphold losses.
Francis Bacon

Misfortunes tell us what fortune is.
Thomas Fuller

Cast away care, he that loves sorrow
Lengthens not a day, nor can buy tomorrow;
Money is trash, and he that will spend it,
Let him drink merrily, fortune will send it.

Thomas Dekker

There is nothing keeps longer than a middling fortune, and nothing melts away sooner than a great one. Poverty treads on the heels of great and unexpected riches.

Jean de La Bruỳere

Wealth can be accumulated but to a slight degree, and communities really live, as the vast majority of individuals live, from hand to mouth. Wealth will not bear much accumulation; except in a few unimportant forms it will not keep.

Henry George

I can afford $100,000 a year for twenty-five years, but no more than that. I don't want to get into a business that's going to lose money permanently.

Sam Gordon

It's a grand thing to be able to take up your money in your hand and to think no more of it when it slips away from you than you would of a trout that would slip back into the stream.

Lady Gregory

The real measure of our wealth is how much we'd be worth if we lost all our money.

John Henry Jowett

Money is mourned with deeper sorrow than friends or kindred.

Juvenal

Riches are gotten with pain, kept with care, and lost with grief.

Thomas Fuller

Nothing stings more deeply, than the loss of money.

Livy

It's good to have money to buy the things that money can buy, but it's better not to lose the things money cannot buy.

George Horace Lorimer

(Money is) something that talks. Most of us can't keep it long enough to hear what it says.

Jimmy Lyons

If you want to know what a man is really like, take notice how he acts when he loses money.

New England proverb

Dame Fortune is a fickle gypsy,
And always blind, and often tipsy.

W.M. Praed

If making money is a slow process, losing it is quickly done.

Ihara Saikaku

There was a time when a fool and his money were soon parted, but now it happens to everybody.

Adlai Stevenson

Money is like an eel in the hand.

Welsh proverb

Love

Kisses may be the language of love, but money still does the talking.

Anonymous

Money cannot buy love, but it can put you in a good bargaining position.

Anonymous

Money cannot buy
The fuel of love
but is excellent kindling.

W.H. Auden

The chase of gain is rich in hate.

Confucius

Loveless men cannot bear need long, they cannot bear fortune long. Loving hearts find peace in love; clever heads find profit in it.

Confucius

Love is the grandest thing on God's earth, but fortunate the lover who has plenty of money.

Russell H. Conwell

What better proof of love can there be than money? A ten shilling note shows incontrovertibly just how mad about you a man is.

Quentin Crisp

Money will say more in one moment than the most eloquent lover can in years.

Henry Fielding

Of all the icy blasts that blow on love, a request for money is the most chilling and havoc-wreaking.

Gustave Flaubert

(Money is) the sinew of love as well as of war.

Thomas Fuller

Women prefer poverty with love to luxury without it.

Haggadah

Knowledge only on the surface; love bought for money; food at the expense of another; these are three miseries of men.

Hitopadesa

The thrill of making a fast buck follows only the thrill of love at first sight. Everyone needs to take an occasional fling with money . . . and with love.

Eliot Janeway

I've had an exciting life. I married for love and got a little money along with it.

Rose Kennedy

When there was enough money for their needs, the ties between them had been strong, but once the money was lacking, what a strain was put on their love!

Gabrielle Roy

Love is the true means by which the world is enjoyed: our love to others, and others' love to us.

Thomas Traherne

Love, pain, and money cannot be kept secret.

Spanish proverb

In love, money shared increases love; money given kills it.

Stendhal

Love is the only gold.

Alfred Lord Tennyson

Some people are more turned on by money than they are by love . . . In one respect they're alike. They're both wonderful as long as they last.

Abigail Van Buren

Love of Money

The love of money is the root of all evil.

The Bible

Love of money is the root of half the evil in the world, and lack of money is the root of the other half.

Anonymous

When you come to analyze the love of money which was the general impulse to effort in your day, you find that the dread of want and desire of luxury were two of several motives which the pursuit of money represented; the others, and with many the more influential, being desire of power, of social position and reputation for ability and success.

Edward Bellamy

Stay away from the love of money; be satisfied with what you have. For God has said, "I will never, never fail you nor forsake you."

The Bible

Jesus said unto him, if thou wilt be perfect, go and sell that thou hast, and give to the poor, and thou shalt have treasure in heaven: and come and follow me. But when the young men heard that saying, he went away sorrowful: for he had great possessions.

Then said Jesus unto his disciples, Verily I say unto you, That a rich man shall hardly enter into the kingdom of heaven.

And again I say unto you, It is easier for a camel to go through the eye of a needle, than for a rich man to enter into the kingdom of God.

When his disciples heard it, they were exceedingly amazed, saying, Who then can be saved?

The Bible

I've been in trouble all my life, I've done the most unutterable rubbish, all because of money. . . . The lure of the zeros was simply too great.

Richard Burton

The more money you have, the harder it is to part with it.

"The Chofetz Chaim"

Still as of old, men by themselves are priced—
For thirty pieces Judas sold himself, not Christ.

Hester H. Cholmondeley

Beware of an inordinate desire for wealth. Nothing is so revealing of narrowness and littleness of soul than love for money. Conversely, there is nothing more honorable or noble than indifference to money, if one doesn't have any; or then genuine altruism and well-doing if one does have it.

Cicero

The wealth he (Jesus) bade his questioner renounce must be taken in a spiritual sense; it was a wealth of passions, a brood of sins in the soul, not money itself, but the love of money.

Saint Clement of Alexandria

I love money. The origin of this joy of money is my Spanish mysticism. In the Middle Ages the alchemists wanted everything they touched to turn to gold. This is the best kind of spiritualization.

Salvador Dali

Every child was taught from his cradle that money was Mammon, the chief agent of the flesh and the devil. As he grew up it was his duty as a Christian and a gentleman to appear to despise filthy lucre, whatever his secret opinion of it might be.

Rebecca Harding Davis

He made money . . . because he honestly loved it with an innocent affection. He was true to it. The reason you have no money is because you don't love it for itself alone. Money won't ever surrender to such a flirt.

Finley Peter Dunne

If you make money your god, it will plague you like the devil.

Henry Fielding

Men make counterfeit money; in many more cases, money makes counterfeit men.

Sydney J. Harris

Wealth is the conjuror's devil,
Whom, when he thinks he hath, the Devil hath him.

George Herbert

The mortal problem of our age is concerned with the love of money, with the habitual appeal to the money motive in nine-tenths of the activities of life.

John Maynard Keynes

Do you wonder that no one tender you the affection which you do not merit, since you prefer your money to everything else?

Horace

The populace may hiss me, but when I go home and think of my money I applaud myself.

Horace

Money swore an oath that nobody who did not love it should ever have it.

Irish proverb

The Almighty Dollar, that great object of universal devotion.

Washington Irving

No man but a blockhead ever wrote except for money.

Samuel Johnson

The love of money has been in all ages, one of the passions that have given great disturbances to the tranquility of the world.

Samuel Johnson

Callous greed grows pious very fast.

Lillian Hellman

The love of money as a possession—as distinguished from the love of money as a means to the enjoyments and realities of life—will be recognized for what it is, a somewhat disgusting morbidity, one of those semi-criminal semi-pathological propensities which one hands over with a shuddle to the specialists in mental disease.

John Maynard Keynes

The two most beautiful words in the English language are 'Cheque Enclosed'.

Dorothy Parker

Love of gain has contaminated many people. There are even occasions when it is better to lose than to gain.

Plautus

Mother, I have given in to wealth: he is my lover, and I his.
Thus from pure affection comes a golden stream!

Francisco de Quevedo

We would rather be rich than famous. That is, more rich and slightly less famous.

John Lennon

In our rich consumers' civilization we spin cocoons around ourselves and get possessed by our possessions.

Max Lerner

The love of money is a form of infantilism. The man who loves money is the man who has never grown up. He has never passed from the world of fairy tales into the world of philosophy.

Robert Lynd

Money is not an aphrodisiac: the desire it may kindle in the female eye is more for the cash than the carrier.

Maria Mannes

There is nothing so habit-forming as money.

Don Marquis

Gentlemen prefer bonds.

Andrew Mellon

We do great injustice to Iscariot, in thinking him wicked above all common wickedness. He was only a common money-lover, and like all money-lovers, did not understand Christ.

John Ruskin

The most grievous kind of destination is to want money in the midst of wealth.

Seneca

The love of money is the root of all virtue.

George Bernard Shaw

Some men worship rank, some worship heroes, some worship God, and over these ideals they dispute—but they all worship money.

Mark Twain

The universal regard for money is the one hopeful fact in our civilization.

George Bernard Shaw

. . . money . . . is really the difference between men and animals, most of the things men feel animals feel and vice versa, but animals do not know about money, money is purely a human conception and that is very important to know, very very important.

Gertrude Stein

It is a rather pleasant experience to be alone in a bank at night.

Willie Sutton

A diamond is the only kind of ice that keeps a girl warm.

Elizabeth Taylor

Once poor, always wanting'. Rich is just a way of wantin' bigger.

Lily Tomlin

All those men have their price.

Robert Walpole

O sacred hunger of pernicious gold!
What bands of faith can impious lucre hold?

Virgil

Most men's hearts are located rather closer to their britch pockets than they are to their breast pockets.

Edward Noyes Westcott

Many good qualities are not sufficient to balance a single want—the want of money.

Zimmermann

Luck

Fortunes . . . come tumbling into some men's laps.

Francis Bacon

Here we are sitting in a shower of gold, with nothing to hold up but a pitchfork.

Jules Bertillon

Wealth is an application of mind to nature; and the art of getting rich consists not in industry, much less in saving, but in a better order, a timeliness, in being at the right spot.

Ralph Waldo Emerson

Be not concerned if thou findest thyself in possession of unexpected wealth; Allah will provide an unexpected use for it.

James Jeffrey Roche

To him who has, more shall be given.

German proverb

It isn't enough for you to love money—it's also necessary that money should love you.

Baron Rothschild

From fortune to misfortune is but a step; from misfortune to fortune is a long way.

Yiddish proverb

M

Maintenance
Management
Marriage
Mastery
Materialism
Millionaires
Miserliness
Misery

Maintenance

Let us keep a firm grip upon our money, for without it the whole assembly of virtues are but as blades of grass.

Bhartrihari

It is not large funds that are wanted, but a constant supply, like a small stream that never dies. To have a great capital is not so necessary as to know how to manage a small one and never be without a little.

William Cooper

We all know how the size of sums of money appears to vary in a remarkable way according as they are being paid in or paid out.

Julian Huxley

I glory
More in the cunning purchase of my wealth
Than in the glad possession.

Ben Jonson

Once you have decided to keep a certain pile, it is no longer yours; for you can't spend it.

Michel de Montaigne

Amongst all other things of the world, take care of thy estate, which thou shalt ever preserve, if thou observe three things; first, that thou know what thou hast, what every thing is worth that thou hast; and to see that thou art not wasted by thy servants and officers.

Walter Raleigh

For many men, the acquisition of wealth does not end their troubles, it only changes them.

Seneca

Management

Taking it with you isn't nearly so important as making it last until you're ready to go.

Anonymous

As far as you can possibly, pay ready money for everything you buy, and avoid bills. . . . Where you must have bills (as for meat and drink, clothes, etc.), pay them regularly every month, and with your own hand. Never, from a mistaken economy, buy a thing you do not want because it is cheap, or, from a silly pride, because it is dear. Keep an account in a book of all that you receive, and of all that you pay; for no man, who knows what he receives and what he pays, ever runs out.

Earl of Chesterfield

Economy means management and nothing more. The most liberal disposition, a disposition precisely the contrary to that of the miser, is perfectly consistent with economy.

William Cobbett

Abundance is a blessing to the wise;
The use of riches in discretion lies;
Learn this, ye men of wealth—a heavy purse
In a fool's pocket is a heavy curse.

Richard Cumberland

The secret and the difference between winners and losers is in discipline. The winner manages his money. The loser lets the money manage him.

Nicholas Dandalos

If anything is evident about people who manage money, it is that the task attracts a very low level of talent, one that is protected in its highly imperfect profession by the mystery that is thought to enfold the subject of economics in general and of money in particular.

John Kenneth Galbraith

Many people take no care of their money till they come nearly to the end of it, and others do just the same with their time.

Johann W. von Goethe

To acquire wealth is not easy, yet to keep it is even more difficult. . . . It is said that wealth is like a viper which is harmless if a man know how to take hold of it; but, if he does not, it will twine around his hand and bite him.

Frank K. Houston

To have money is good; to have control of money is still better.

Hebrew proverb

With luck and resolution and good guidance . . . the human mind can survive not only poverty, but even wealth.

Gilbert Highet

The mint makes it first, and it's up to us to make it last.

Anonymous

Every young man should have a hobby. Learning how to handle money is the best one.

Jack Hurley

My talent is making money, not managing it.

Norman Mailer

I find it more trouble to take care of money than to get it.

Michel de Montaigne

Just about the time you think you can make both ends meet, somebody moves the ends.

Pansy Penner

Multiplying wealth is by far the fastest way to help the poor. Dividing the wealth and subsidizing poverty is the fastest way to starve everyone.

Paul L. Poirot

Knowing how to make money and also how to keep it; either one of these gifts might make a rich man.

Seneca

Earn a little, and spend a little—less.

John Stevenson

Marriage

The most popular labour-saving device today is still a husband with money.

Joey Adams

Love makes passion, but money makes marriage.

French proverb

Some men don't marry until they find the one girl in a million; others won't until they find the one girl *with* a million.

Anonymous

No married man can understand why every bachelor isn't a millionaire.

Anonymous

If there's one thing better than marrying a millionaire, it's divorcing him.

Anonymous

It is better to marry a man without money than to marry money without a man.

Anonymous

The woman who marries a man for his money will probably divorce him for the same reason.

Anonymous

Marry for love and you divorce for money; marry for money and you divorce for love.

Anonymous

Some people marry for love, some for money, but most for a short time.

Anonymous

If you earn $10,000 a year and your wife earns nothing, she's a dependent; but if she earns $10,000 and you earn nothing, you're a bum.

Anonymous

Money always talks most when a man marries it.

Anonymous

Because the cost of living is so high, it would be wise for many a young man to postpone marriage until she is earning more.

Anonymous

Don't get married on a shoe-string or you may find it hard to stay tied.

Anonymous

If thee marries for money, thee surely will earn it.

Ezra Bowen

All ought to refrain from marriage who cannot avoid abject poverty for their children; for poverty is not only a great evil, but tends to its own increase by leading to recklessness in marriage.

Charles Darwin

He that is needy when he is married,
Shall not be rich when he is buried.

Thomas Fuller

The fellow who waits to get married until he has enough money, isn't really in love.

Kin Hubbard

I always start (writing) a book for money. If you're married five times you have to.

Norman Mailer

Why am I unwilling to marry a rich wife? Do you ask? I will not be given in marriage to my wife.

Martial

Doant thou marry for munny, but goa wheer munny is!

Alfred Lord Tennyson

Mastery

Money is a terrible master but an excellent servant.

P.T. Barnum

Money is a good servant but a bad master.

H.G. Bohn

If we command our wealth, we shall be rich and free; if our wealth commands us, we are poor indeed.

Edmund Burke

(The rich) are indeed rather possessed by their money than possessors.

Robert Buryon

He does not see, poor wretch, that his life is but a gilded torture, that he is bound fast by his wealth, and that his money owns him rather than he owns it.

Cyprian of Carthage

All things, divine and human—virtue, fame, honor—are slaves to the beauty of riches.

Horace

(Money is) Slave or master.

Horace

(Wealth) is a . . . device of fate whereby men are made captive and burdened with responsibilities.

Elbert Hubbard

A credit is worse than a master; for a master owns only your person, a creditor owns your dignity, and can belabour that.

Victor Hugo

It is not the rich man only who is under the dominion of things; they too are slaves who, having no money, are unhappy from the lack of it.

George MacDonald

Luxury makes a man so soft that it is hard to please him, and easy to trouble him; so that his pleasures at last become his burden. Luxury is a nice master, hard to be pleased.

Mackenzie

We can hardly respect money enough for the blood and toil it represents. Money is frightening. It can serve or destroy man.

Michel Quoist

A good mind possesses a kingdom: a great fortune is a great slavery.

Seneca

Money is a new form of slavery, and distinguishable from the old simply by the fact that it is impersonal—that there is no human relation between master and slave.

Leo Tolstoy

Materialism

(Money is) a kind of institutionalized dream which . . . constitutes the main fantasy on which our way of life has been built.

David T. Bazelon

(The dollar is) the only object to worship.

Anonymous

Lay not up for yourselves treasures upon earth.

The Bible

Americans have an abiding belief in their ability to control reality by purely material means. Hence . . . airline insurance replaces the fear of death with the comforting prospect of cash.

Cecil Beaton

But I have learned a thing or two; I know as sure as fate,
When we lock up our lives for wealth, the gold key comes too late.

Will Carleton

(Wealth is) gilded torture.

Saint Cyprian

No government can inoculate its people against the fatal materialism that plagues our age. Happily our people, though blessed with more material goods than any people in history, have always reserved their first allegiance to the kingdom of spirit, which is the true source of that freedom we value above all material things.

Dwight D. Eisenhower

If a man be weighed down with worldliness, he shall sink like an overladen boat in the world's ocean.

Amar Das

Money is just what we use to keep tally.

Henry Ford

We live in a vastly complex society which has been able to provide us with a multitude of material things, and this is good, but people are beginning to suspect that we have paid a high spiritual price for our plenty.

Euell Gibbons

Just how we fit into the plans of the Great Architect and how much He has assigned us to do, we do not know, but if we fail in our assignment it is pretty certain that part of the job will be left undone. But fit in we certainly do somehow, else we would not have a sense of our own responsibility. A purely materialistic philosophy is to me the height of unintelligence.

Robert A. Millikan

A too constant preoccupation with money may seem to indicate the lack of a proper sense of moral values, but (let) those who have always had money . . . be without it for a while, and they will soon discover how quickly it becomes their chief concern.

Moss Hart

Ill fares the land, to hastening ills a prey,
Where wealth accumulates and men decay.

Oliver Goldsmith

Pearls around the neck (may represent) stones upon the heart.

Hebrew Folk Saying

American business needs a lifting purpose greater than the struggle of materialism.

Herbert Hoover

Money breeds insensitiveness.

Aldous Huxley

If Karl, instead of writing a lot about Capital, made a lot of Capital, it would have been much better.

Henrietta Marx
Mother of Karl Marx

Money, money, money do you feel like a pawn in your own world? You found the system and you lost the pearl . . .

Laura Nyro

Posterity will some day laugh at the foolishness of modern materialistic philosophy. The more I study nature, the more I am amazed at the Creator.

Louis Pasteur

It is the preoccupation with possession, more than anything else, that prevents men from living freely and nobly.

Bertrand Russell

For one man robbed on the road, a hundred are robbed at the inn.

Spanish proverb

Millionaires

The only difference between a millionaire and the rest of us is that while he's working on his second million, we're working on our first.

Anonymous

Nobody in football is worth a million dollars! It's ridiculous!

Joe Paterno

The man who claims that poverty and hard word are good for character is usually a millionaire.

Anonymous

The person who minds nobody's business but his own is probably a millionaire.

Anonymous

It is easier for a man to be good for a million than for a million to be good for a man.

Anonymous

Many a woman's dream is to make a millionaire out of a multi-millionaire.

Anonymous

When a millionaire's money talks, it usually talks about more money.

Anonymous

A man who has a million dollars is as well off as if he were rich.

Attributed to
John Jacob Astor III

If you can count your money, you don't have a billion dollars.

J. Paul Getty

It takes a kind of genius to make a fortune, and especially a large fortune. It is neither goodness, nor wit, nor talent, nor strength, nor delicacy. I don't know precisely what it is: I am waiting for some one to tell me.

Jean de la Bruyère

The idea all along was to make a hundred million dollars. Otherwise the struggle wouldn't have been worth it. I have American ideals. I love money.

Alice Cooper

Lampis the shipowner, on being asked how he acquired his great wealth, replied, "My great wealth was acquired with no difficulty, but my small wealth, my first gains, with much labor."

Epictetus

Persons who have never made or saved a dollar are always telling me how to spend a million.

Henry Ford

Nothing is more admirable than the fortitude with which millionaires tolerate the disadvantages of their wealth.

Rex Stout

I had to be a millionaire. If I couldn't do it without being crooked, then I'd have to be crooked.

John Lennon

No woman marries for money: they are all clever enough before marrying a millionaire, to fall in love with him first.

Cesare Pavese

A million dollars is not what it used to be.

Howard Hughes

Viewing the matter in retrospect, I can testify that it is nearly always easier to make one million dollars honestly than to dispose of it wisely.

Julius Rosenwald

The losses of the poor are much harder to repair than those of the rich, and . . . the difficulty of acquisition is always greater in proportion as there is more need for it. "Nothing comes out of nothing," is as true of life as in physics: money is the seed of money, and the first guinea is sometimes more difficult to acquire than the second million.

Henri Rousseau

Miserliness

A miser is a poor wretch who has nothing but money.

Anonymous

A miser begins by saving up for a rainy day, and ends by saving up for the rainy days of his heirs.

Anonymous

The spendthrift is never happy, never satisfied. The man who has saved nothing can seldom seize business opportunities. Many a fortune has been made by ability to seize an opportunity when it presented itself, an opportunity that called for the prompt furnishing of a certain sum of money.

B.C. Forbes

A miser is the proof that not every fool and his money are soon parted.

Anonymous

A miser is known by the money he keeps.

Anonymous

Miserliness is an expensive habit.

"The Chofetz Chaim"

Every man serves a useful purpose: a miser, for example, makes a wonderful ancestor.

Anonymous

I would rather be a beggar and spend my money like a king, then be a king and spend money like a beggar.

Robert G. Ingersoll

A miser is a guy who lives within his income. He's also called a magician.

Alliston Herald

After spending some money in his sleep, Hermon the miser was so hopping mad he hanged himself.

Lucilius

It is folly to live poor and die rich.

Scottish proverb

What good was her money since she deprived herself of everything?

Mme La Comtesse de Segur

Misers are very kind people: they amass wealth for those who wish their death.

Stanislaus, King of Poland

The only right thing a miser can do is die.

Publilius Syrus

Misery

The rich man may never get into heaven, but the pauper is already serving his term in hell.

Alexander Chase

. . . money isn't so hot, after all. What with incipient heart attacks, lots of bottles of little pills you have to take all the time, and losing your temper over the food or the service in hotels. Most of the rich people I've known have been fairly miserable.

Agatha Christie

What good is a silver urn if it is full of tears?

Hebrew proverb

The big majority of Americans, who are comparatively well off, have developed an ability to have enclaves of people living in the greatest misery without almost noticing them.

Gunnar Myrdal

Must the hunger become anger and the anger fury before anything will be done?

John Steinbeck

There is only one class in the community that thinks more about money than the rich, and that is the poor. The poor can think of nothing else. That is the misery of being poor.

Oscar Wilde

N

Necessities

Need

Necessities

A feast is made for laughter, and wine maketh merry: but money answereth all things.

The Bible

(Money): the representative of a certain quality of corn or other commodity. Its value is in the necessities of the animal man. It is so much warmth, so much bread.

Ralph Waldo Emerson

Wealth begins in a tight roof that keep the rain and wind out; in a good pump that yields you plenty of sweet water, in dry sticks to burn, in a good double-wick lamp and three meals. . . . Money often costs too much, and power and pleasure are not cheap.

Ralph Waldo Emerson

"No matter whence the money comes, but money you must have." This is the lesson taught by skinny old nurses to little boys before they can walk; this is what every girl learns before her alphabet.

Juvenal

I've known what it is to be hungry, but I always went right to a restaurant.

Ring Lardner

All forms of government fall when it comes up to the question of bread—bread for the family, something to eat. Bread to a man with a hungry family comes first—before his union, before his citizenship, before his church affiliation. Bread!

John L. Lewis

Money is like a sixth sense, and you can't make use of the other five without it.

William Sommerset Maugham

What riches give us let us then inquire— Meat, fire and clothes. What more? Meat, clothes and fire.

Alexander Pope

Money makes up in a measure all other wants in men.

William Wycherley

Need

You can't take it with you, but where on earth can you go without it?

Anonymous

When a man needs money, he needs money, and not a headache tablet or a prayer.

William Feather

(Money is) a guarantee that we may have what we want in the future. Though we need nothing at the moment, it insures the possibility of satisfying a necessary desire when it arises.

Aristotle

(The) answer was good that Diogenes made to one that asked him in mockery, "How came it to pass that philosophers were the followers of rich men, and not rich men of philosophers?" He answered soberly, and yet sharply, "Because the one sort knew what they have need of, and the other did not."

Francis Bacon

A poor man with nothing in his belly needs hope, illusion, more than bread.

Georges Bernanos

A man without money is a bow without an arrow.

Thomas Fuller

But for money and the need of it, there would not be half the friendship in the world. It is powerful for good if divinely used. Give it plenty of air and it is sweet as the hawthorn; shut it up and it cankers and breeds worms.

George MacDonald

To write songs, I usually need a reason. Like not having any money.

Willie Nelson

The man has the burden of the money. It's needed day after day. More and more of it. For ordinary things and for life. That's why holidays are a hard time for him. Another hard time is the weekend, when he's not making money or furthering himself.

Grace Paley

There is a vast difference in some instances between what we really need and that which we think we must have, and the realization of this truth will greatly lessen the seeming discomfort in doing without.

William M. Peck

Advertising is designed to create, and does create, dissatisfaction . . . Advertising intended for an audience that can afford what it offers also works . . . on those who cannot afford it; it inflames the desires of the poor without offering them any satisfaction at all. Perhaps the poor are "better off than ever before," as some say, but they can hardly be expected to be satisfied with this after watching television . . . Television might justly be called a riot box.

Charles A. Reich

(Wealth is) to have what is necesary; and, secondly, to have what is enough.

Seneca

O

Obsession
Ostentation

Obsession

Money is the last enemy that shall never be subdued. While there is flesh there is money—or the want of money, but money is always on the brain so long as there is a brain in reasonable order.

Samuel Butler

The moral problem of our age is concerned with the love of money, with the habitual appeal to the money motive in nine-tenths of the activities of life.

J.M. Keynes

He worked like hell in the country so he could live in the city, where he worked like hell so he could live in the country.

Don Marquis

(Riches are) the incentives to evil.

Ovid

Whenever money is the principal object of life with either man or nation, it is both got ill, and spent ill; and does harm both in the getting and spending.

John Ruskin

It is physically impossible for a well-educated, intellectual, or brave man to make money the chief object of his thoughts.

John Ruskin

In democratic countries, however opulent a man is supposed to be, he is almost always discontented with his fortune because he finds that he is less rich than his father was, and he fears that his sons will be less rich than himself. Most rich men in democracies are therefore constantly haunted by the desire of obtaining wealth, and they naturally turn their attention to trade and manufactures, which appear to offer the readiest and most efficient means of success. In this respect they share the instincts of the poor without feeling the same necessities; say, rather, they fell the most imperious of all necessities, that of not sinking in the world.

Alexis de Tocqueville

Ostentation

Money never made a fool of anybody; it only shows 'em up.

Kin Hubbard

For a man to pride himself on this kind of wealth, as if it enriched him, is as ridiculous as if one struggling in the ocean with a bag of gold on his back should gasp out, "I am worth a hundred thousand dollars!" I see his ineffectual struggles just as plainly, and what it is that sinks him.

Thoreau

No man divulges his revenue, or at least which way it comes in; but everyone publishes his acquisitions.

Michel de Montaigne

The insolence of wealth will creep out.

Samuel Johnson

With the great part of rich people, the chief employment of riches consists in the parade of riches.

Adam Smith

As regards our own welfare, there are only two ways in which we can use wealth. We can either spend it in ostentatious pomp, and feed on the cheap respect which our imaginary glory will bring us from the infatuated crowed; or, by avoiding all expenditure that will do us no good, we can let our wealth grow, so that we may have a bulwark against misfortune and want that shall be stronger and better every day.

Schopenhauer

P

People

Philanthropy

Politics

Poverty

Power

Presidents on Money

Pride

Principles

Production

Profit

Property

Prosperity

Prudence

People

There are two types of people: those who cannot make it, and those who cannot keep it.

Anonymous

The only thing I like about rich people is their money.

Lady Astor

Believe not much them that seem to despise riches; for they despise them that despair of them; and none worse, when they come to them.

Francis Bacon

If all the rich men in the world divided up their money amongst themselves, there wouldn't be enough to go around.

Jules Bertillon

The gods are those who either have money or do not want it.

Samuel Butler

I went into the business for the money, and the art grew out of it. If people are disillusioned by that remark, I can't help it. It's the truth.

Charlie Chaplin

After I decided to become a Jew only then did I learn the Jews don't really have all the money. When I found out Rockefeller and Ford were goyim I almost resigned.

Sammy Davis, Jr.

There are people who have money and people who are rich.

Coco Chanel

(Wealth is) the savings of many in the hands of one.

Eugene V. Debs

As a general rule, nobody has money who ought to have it.

Benjamin Disraeli

Let me tell you about the very rich. They are different from you and me. They possess and enjoy early, and it does something to them, makes them soft where we are hard, and cynical where we are trustful, in a way that, unless you were born rich, it is very difficult to understand.

F. Scott Fitzgerald

God gave me my money.

John D. Rockefeller

People who know how much they're worth aren't usually worth that much.

Nelson Bunker Hunt

I wake up at two, sometimes at three. First is my massage. Afterwards I answer my phone calls and see my bankers, racing managers and lawyers—the usual daily chores.

The Maharanee of Baroda

The wealthy man is the man who *is* much, not the one who has much.

Karl Marx

After the rich, the most obnoxious people in the world are those who serve the rich.

Edna O'Brien

I don't have any money. I have exactly $5,200 in a bank account.

Jacqueline Kennedy Onassis

I consider it my patriotic duty to keep Elvis in the 90-percent tax bracket.

Tom Parker

When people suddenly become prosperous, they also become preposterous.

Laurence J. Peter

I'd like to live like a poor man with lots of money.

Pablo Picasso

The matter, form, effect, and goal of riches are worthless. That's why our Lord God generally gives riches to crude asses to whom he doesn't give anything else.

Martin Luther

We may see the small value God has for riches by the people he gives them to.

Alexander Pope

The vast wealth which Stephen Girard had was itself alone evidence of greatness.

Thomas B. Reed

"But after all, what's money?"
"Nothing, of course," said Peter, "But if you've been brought up to havin' it, it's a bit awkward to drop it suddenly. Like baths, you know."

Dorothy L. Sayers

It is the wretchedness of being rich that you have to live with rich people.

Logan Pearsall Smith

If someone is dumb enough to offer me a million dollars to make a picture—I am certainly not dumb enough to turn it down.

Elizabeth Taylor

Philanthropy

As to world riches, if you do not possess them, let them not be sought after on earth by doing evil; and if you possess them, let them by good works be paid up in heaven.

Saint Augustine

Money-getters are the benefactors of our race. To them . . . are we indebted for our institutions of learning, and of art, our academies, colleges, and churches.

P. T. Barnum

Philanthropist: a rich (and usually bald) old gentleman who has trained himself to grin while his conscience is picking his pocket.

Ambrose Bierce

Money: A blessing that is of no advantage to us excepting when we part with it.

Ambrose Bierce

A man's true wealth is the good he does in this world.

Mohammed

The making of money, the accumulation of material power, is not all there is to living. Life is something more than these, and the man who misses this truth misses the greatest joy and satisfaction that can come into his life—service for others.

Edward Bok

Money is the symbol of duty, it is the sacrament of having done for mankind that which mankind wanted.

Samuel Butler

At the end, the acquisition of wealth is ignoble in the extreme. I assume that you save and long for wealth only as a means of enabling you the better to do some good in your day and generation.

Andrew Carnegie

What is the poor pride arising from a magnificent house, a numerous equipage, a splendid table, and from all the other advantages or appearances of fortune, compared to the warm, solid content, the swelling satisfaction, the thrilling transports, and the exulting triumphs, which a good mind enjoys, in the contemplation of a generous, virtuous, noble, benevolent action?

Henry Fielding

No man giveth, but with intention of good to himself; because the gift is voluntary, and of all voluntary acts the object is to every man his own good.

Thomas Hobbes

No man who continues to add something to the material, intellectual and moral well-being of the place in which he lives is left long without proper reward.

Booker T. Washington

(Riches) A sort of duty . . . that it may be in one's power to do good.

Mary W. Montagu

Make all you can, save all you can, give all you can.

John Wesley

Politics

In politics, as in high finance, duplicity is regarded as a virtue.

Mikhail A. Bakunin

Money speaks sense in a language all nations understand.

Aphra Behn

We have among us a class of mammon worshippers, whose one test of conservatism or radicalism is the attitude one takes with respect to accumulated wealth. Whatever tends to preserve the wealth of the wealthy is called conservatism, and whatever favors anything else, no matter what, they call socialism.

Richard T. Ely

As restrictions and prohibitions are multiplied the people grow poorer and poorer. When they are subjected to overmuch government, the land is thrown into confusion.

Lao-Tzu

Money makes the mayor go.

Oliver Herford

If you destroy the leisure class, you destroy civilization.

J. P. Morgan

Luxury is the first, second and third cause of the ruin of republics. It is the vampire which soothes us into a fatal slumber while it sucks the life-blood of our veins.

Payson

Just be glad you're not getting all the government you're paying for.

Will Rogers

Politics has got so expensive that it takes lots of money to even get beat with.

Will Rogers

Money is the mother's milk of politics.

Jesse Unruh

In all well-instituted commonwealths, care has been taken to limit men's possessions; which is done for many reasons, and, among the rest, for one which, perhaps, is not often considered, that when bounds are set to men's desires, after they have acquired as much as the laws will permit them, their private interests is at an end, and they have nothing to do but to take care of the public.

Jonathan Swift

A disordered currency is one of the greatest political evils.

Daniel Webster

Knowledge—Zzzzzp! Money—Zzzzzp! Power! That's the cycle democracy is built on!

Tennessee Williams

Poverty

Poverty is the parent of revolution and crime.

Aristotle

A very narrow income has a tendency to contract the mind and sour the temper. Those who can barely live, and who live perforce in a very small and generally inferior society, may well be illiberal and cross.

Jane Austen

Poverty is an anomaly to rich people: it is very difficult to make out why people who want dinner do not ring the bell.

Walter Bagehot

Neither great poverty nor great riches will hear reason.

Henry Fielding

Loneliness and the feeling of being unwanted is the most terrible poverty.

Mother Teresa

What mean ye that ye beat my people to pieces and grind the faces of the poor?

The Bible

There are many in this old world of ours who hold that things break about even for all of us. I have observed for example that we all get the same amount of ice. The rich get it in the summertime and the poor get it in the winter.

Bat Masterson

A man isn't poor if he can still laugh.

Raymond Hitchcock

Blessed be ye poor: for yours is the Kingdom of God.

The Bible

Poverty is very good in poems, but it is very bad in a house. It is very good in maxims and in sermons, but it is very bad in practical life.

Henry Ward Beecher

For ye have the poor always with you.

The Bible

Six long months have passed
Since I have slept in bed.
I ain't eat a square meal o' vittles in three long weeks;
Money thinks I'm dead.

Black American Song

Money gives an appearance of beauty even to ugliness; but everything becomes frightful with poverty.

Nicolas Boileau

When I was running about this town a very poor fellow, I was a great arguer for the advantages of poverty; but I was, at the same time, very sorry to be poor. . . . All the arguments which are brought to represent poverty as no evil, show it to be evidently a great evil. You never find people labouring to convince you that you may live very happily upon a plentiful fortune.

James Boswell

The great curse of our modern society is not so much the lack of money as the fact that the lack of money condemns a man to a squalid and incomplete existence.

Christopher Dawson

He that is without money might as well be buried in rice with his mouth sewed up.

Chinese proverb

If you have no money, be polite.

Danish proverb

The heaviest baggage for a traveler is an empty purse.

English proverb

There is no scandal like rags, nor any crime so shameful as poverty.

George Farquhar

Poverty is no vice, but an inconvenience.

John Florio

A man without money is like a wolf without teeth.

French proverb

If I were convinced that by giving away my fortune I could make a real contribution toward solving the problems of world poverty, I'd give away 99.5 percent of all I have immediately.

J. Paul Getty

The conspicuously wealthy turn up urging the character-building value of privation for the poor.

John Kenneth Galbraith

The poor man must suffer for the rich man's transgressions.

German proverb

. . . in England, having had money . . . is just as acceptable as having it, since the upperclass mannerisms persist, even after the bankroll has disappeared. But never having had money is unforgivable, and can only be atoned for by never trying to get any.

Margaret Halsey

The best way to help the poor is not to become one of them.

Laing Hancock

Boredom is the keynote of poverty . . . for where there is no money there is no change of any kind, not of scene or of routine.

Moss Hart

Poverty in itself does not make men into a rabble; a rabble is created only when there is joined to poverty a disposition of mind, an inner indignation against the rich, against society, against the government, etc.

Georg W. Hegel

It's no disgrace to be poor, but it's no honor, either.

Hebrew proverb

The heaviest weight in the world is an empty pocket.

Hebrew proverb

It's not that money makes everything good; it's that no money makes everything rotten.

Hebrew proverb

Hope is the poor man's bread.

George Herbert

Poverty must have many satisfactions, else there would not be so many poor people.

Don Herold

And when you're poor, you grow up fast.

Billie Holiday

A single solitary philosopher may be great, virtuous and happy in the depth of poverty, but not a whole people.

Iselin

Poverty indeed is the strenuous life,—without brass bands or uniforms or hysteric popular applause or lies or circumlocutions.

William James

In the prospect of poverty there is nothing but gloom and melancholy; the mind and body suffer together; its miseries bring no alleviations; it is a state in which every virtue is obscured, and in which no conduct can avoid reproach; a state in which cheerfulness is insensibility, and dejection sullenness, of which the hardships are without honor, and the labors without reward.

Samuel Johnson

Poverty has, in large cities, very different appearances: it is often concealed in splendour, and often in extravagance. It is the care of a very great part of mankind to conceal their indigence from the rest: they support themselves by temporary expedients, and every day is lost in contriving for the morrow.

Samuel Johnson

He who knows how to be poor knows everything.

Jules Michelet

Poverty takes away so many means of doing good, and produces so much inability to resist evil, both natural and moral, that it is by all virtuous means to be avoided.

Samuel Johnson

Poverty's greatest curse, much worse than the fact of it, is that it makes men objects of mirth, reduced, humbled, embarrassed.

Juvenal

Fortune never seems so blind as to those upon whom she has bestowed no favors.

La Rochefoucauld

Of all the preposterous assumptions of humanity over humanity, nothing exceeds most of the criticisms made on the habits of the poor by the well-housed, well-warmed, and well-fed.

Herman Melville

Put all other sufferings in one side of the scale, and poverty in the other, and poverty would be heavier.

Midrash

The poor ye have with ye always—but they are not invited.

Addison Mizner

The child was diseased at birth, stricken with a hereditary ill that only the most vital men are able to shake off. I mean poverty—the most deadly and prevalent of all diseases.

Eugene O'Neill

Rattle his bones over the stones!
He's only a pauper, whom nobody owns!

T. Noel

Few have too much and fewer too little.

Norwegian proverb

Short of genius, a rich man cannot imagine poverty.

Charles Peguy

Those who escape from destitution do not escape from the memory of their destitution. Either by dwelling upon it or by reacting against it, all their future life is affected by it. The majority of the once destitute take refuge in voluntary amnesia.

Charles Peguy

I absolutely disagree with the theory that you can upgrade the poor by giving them better housing.

Kevin P. Phillips

Poverty is dishonourable not in itself, but when it is a proof of laziness, intemperance, luxury, and carelessness; whereas in a person that is temperate, industrious, just, and valiant, and who uses all his virtues for the public good, it shows a great and lofty mind.

Plutarch

He was naturally subject to a kind of disease, which at that time they called lack of money.

François Rabelais

Wealth is conspicuous, but poverty hides.

James Reston

The chief problem of the lower-income farmers is poverty.

Nelson Rockefeller

Whereas it has long been known and declared that the poor have no right to the property of the rich, I wish it also to be known and declared that the rich have no right to the property of the poor.

John Ruskin

Poverty does not produce unhappiness: it produces degradation.

George Bernard Shaw

. . . the poor are our brothers and sisters . . . (They are the) people in the world who need love, who need care, who have to be wanted.

Mother Teresa

Poverty is a bully if you are afraid of her, or truckle to her. Poverty is good-natured if you meet her like a man.

W. M. Thackeray

Where I was brought up we never talked about money because there was never enough to furnish a topic of conversation.

Mark Twain

When a poor man eats a chicken, one or the other is sick.

Yiddish proverb

Power

Money talks, but not when it's a small amount.

Anonymous

(A dollar is) a soldier that does your bidding.

Vincent Astor

A man who is furnished with arguments from the mint will convince his antagonist much sooner than one who draws them from reason and philosophy.

Joseph Addison

Wine maketh merry: but money answereth all things.

The Bible

He who has his thumb on the purse has the power.

Otto Von Bismark

As wealth is power, so all power will infallibly draw wealth to itself by some means or other.

Edmund Burke

Gold: A ruthless king is he.

Henry F. Chorley

Money is more eloquent than a dozen members of Parliament.

Danish proverb

To be rich is to have a ticket of admission to the masterworks and chief men of each race.

Ralph Waldo Emerson

(Wealth is) the thing most honored among men, and the source of the greatest power.

Euripides

The world is his who has money to go over it.

Ralph Waldo Emerson

The rich need not beg a welcome.

French proverb

Mention money and the whole world is silent.

German proverb

A rich man, though foolish, is treated like a lord.

Hebrew folk saying

Money has no legs, but it runs.

Japanese proverb

Wealth may be an excellent thing, for it means power, it means leisure, it means liberty.

James Russell Lowell

But it is pretty to see what money will do.

Samuel Pepys

The force of the guinea you have in your pocket depends wholly on the default of a guinea in your neighbor's pocket. If he did not want it, it would be of no use to you.

John Ruskin

When you've got them by the wallets, their hearts and minds will follow.

Verne Naito

(Money is) the cause of good things to a good man, or evil things to a bad man.

Philo

When money speaks, the truth keeps silent.

Russian proverb

Money is the most egalitarian force in society. It confers power on whoever holds it.

Roger Starr

Money alone sets all the world in motion.

Publilius Syrus

The door will not open to words, and it is only a well-filled palm that should do the knocking.

Tibullus

Presidents on Money

We have not yet reached the goal but . . . we shall soon, with the help of God, be in sight of the day when poverty shall be banished from this nation.

Herbert Hoover

This administration here and now declares unconditional war on poverty in America.

Lyndon B. Johnson

Our purpose is not to buy friends or hire allies. Our purpose is to defeat poverty . . . Our goal is to again influence history instead of merely observing it.

John F. Kennedy

The society of excess profits for some and small returns for others, the society in which a few prey upon the many, the society in which few took advantage and many took great disadvantage, must pass.

Wendell L. Willkie

The great monopoly in this country is the money monopoly. So long as it exists, our old variety of freedom and individual energy of development are out of the question.

Woodrow Wilson

If a free society cannot help the many who are poor, it cannot save the few that are rich.

John F. Kennedy

This land of ours cannot be a good place for any of us to live in unless we make it a good place for all of us to live in.

Richard M. Nixon

Pride

The prouder a man is, the more he thinks he deserves; and the more he thinks he deserves, the less he really does deserve.

Henry Ward Beecher

Proud of your money you may strut,
But fortune does not change your birth.

Horace

One of the surprising things of this world is the respect a worthless man has for himself.

Ed Howe

Make money, be proud of it; make more money, be prouder of it.

Henry Luce

Where wealth is, there are also all manner of sins; for through wealth comes pride, through pride, dissension, through dissension, wars, through wars, poverty, through poverty, great distress and misery. Therefore, they that are rich, must yield a strict and great account; for to whom much is given, of him will much be required.

Martin Luther

He that is proud of riches is a fool. For if he be exalted above his neighbors because he hath more gold, how much inferior is he to a gold mine.

Jeremy Taylor

Have more than thou showest,
Speak less than thou knowest.

Shakespeare

If ever a man becomes proud, let him remember that a mosquito preceded him in the divine order of creation!

Tosefta

Principles

When a fellow says, "It ain't the money but the principle of the thing," it's the money.

Kin Hubbard

Money is only money, beans tonight and steak tomorrow. So long as you can look yourself in the eye.

Meridel Le Sueur

First as to his fortune, for the last question that will be asked will be as to his morals.

Juvenal

Moral principle is a looser bond than pecuniary interest.

Abraham Lincoln

What happens to man is less significant than what happens within him.

Thomas Mann

Rich men without convictions are more dangerous in modern society than poor women without chastity.

George Bernard Shaw

Trying to live without money is easier than trying to live without convictions.

Roy L. Smith

Production

It's just as well that you can't come back and see what they've done with what you couldn't take with you.

Anonymous

Psychologically I should say that a person becomes an adult at the point when he produces more than he consumes or earns more than he spends. This may be at the age of eighteen, twenty-five, or thirty-five. Some people remain unproductive and dependent children forever and therefore intellectually and emotionally immature.

Henry C. Link

Profit

Business without profit is not business any more than a pickle is a candy.

Charles F. Abbott

In business, the earning of profit is something more than an incident of success. It is an essential condition of success. It is an essential condition of success because the continued absence of profit itself spells failure.

Louis D. Brandeis

It is a socialist idea that making profits is a vice; I consider the real vice is making losses.

Winston Churchill

Profitability is the sovereign criterion of the enterprise.

Peter Drucker

The worst crime against the working people is a company which fails to make a profit.

Samuel Gompers

The only way to keep score in business is to add up how much money you make.

Harry Helmsley

Where profit is, loss is hidden nearby.

Japanese proverb

No man profiteth but by the loss of others.

Michel de Montaigne

If you count all your assets you always show a profit.

Robert Quillen

Property

People who never had enough thrift and forethought to buy and pay for property in the first place seldom have enough to keep the property up after they have gained it in some other way.

Thomas Nixon Carver

Well! Some people talk of morality, and some of religion, but give me a little snug property.

Maria Edgeworth

Men honor property above all else;
it has the greatest power in human life.

Euripides

How can you trust people who are poor and own no property? Inequality of property will exist as long as liberty exists.

Alexander Hamilton

What we call real estate—the solid ground to build a house on—is the broad foundation on which nearly all of the guilt of the world rests.

Nathaniel Hawthorne

Prosperity

They who prosper take on airs of vanity.

Aeschylus

A prosperous fool is a grievous burden.

Aeschylus

Money isn't everything—for one thing, it isn't plentiful.

Anonymous

Wealthy men are insolent and arrogant; their possession of wealth affects their understanding; they feel as if they had every good thing that exists; wealth becomes a sort of standard of value for everything else, and therefore they imagine there is nothing it cannot buy . . . In a word, the type of character produced by wealth is that of a prosperous fool.

Aristotle

It is a sign of weakness not to bear prosperity as well as adversity with moderation.

Cicero

In prosperity, when the stream of life flows according to our wishes, let us diligently avoid all arrogance, haughtiness and pride.

Cicero

When prosperity comes, do not use all of it.

Confucius

Prosperity is only an instrument to be used, not a deity to be worshipped.

Calvin Coolidge

Prosperity can change man's nature; and seldom is any one cautious enough to resist the effects of good fortune.

Quintus Curtius

And you shall find the greatest enemy
A man can have in his prosperity.

Samuel Daniel

Can anybody remember when the times were not hard, and money not scarce?

Ralph Waldo Emerson

Prosperity is like a tender mother, but blind, who spoils her children.

English proverb

The man who works for the gold in the job rather than for the money in the pay envelope, is the fellow who gets on.

Joseph French Johnson

The prosperous man is never sure that he is loved for himself.

Lucan

Prosperity is a great teacher; adversity is a greater.

William Hazlitt

The fundamental evil of the world arose from the fact that the good Lord has not created money enough.

Heinrich Heine

Remember that there is nothing stable in human affairs; therefore avoid undue elation in prosperity, or undue depression in adversity.

Isocrates

Prosperity must be sensibly restrained or it crushes you.

Latin proverb

I should like to bring a case to trial;
Prosperity versus Beauty,
Cash registers teetering in a balance
against the comfort of the soul.

Amy Lowell

The old thought that one cannot be rich except at the expense of his neighbor, must pass away. True prosperity adds to the richness of the whole world, such as that of the man who makes two trees grow where only one grew before. The parasitical belief in prosperity as coming by the sacrifices of others has no place in the mind that thinks true. "My benefit is your benefit, your success is my success," should be the basis of all our wealth.

Anne Rix Miltz

So long as a man enjoys prosperity, he cares not whether he is beloved.

Lucan

Everything in the world may be endured except continual prosperity.

Johann W. von Goethe

Receive wealth or prosperity without arrogance; and be ready to let it go.

Marcus Aurelius

Prosperity of the middling and lower orders depends upon the fortunes and light taxes of the rich.

Andrew Mellon

Exclusiveness is a characteristic of recent riches, high society, and the skunk.

Austin O'Malley

Spend all you can; never mind what your husband says: that is the best way to spread prosperity.

Charles M. Schwab

Plenty is the child of peace.

William Prynne

A man is insensible to the relish of prosperity
Till he has tasted adversity.

Sa'Di

Nothing knits man to man like the frequent passage from hand to hand of cash.

Walter Sickert

All men, when prosperity is at its height, ought then chiefly to consider in what way they will endure disaster.

Terence

Prudence

Do not give up in despair because you have a small income, and resign yourself to living meanly, in a hand to mouth fashion. Self-denial and saving and resolute abstention from luxuries will solve the problem.

Mary Hinman Abel

He frivols through the livelong day,
He knows not Poverty, her pinch.

Franklin P. Adams

Nowadays it seems that the miser is the only one who lives within his means.

Anonymous

Money talks, but it doesn't always talk sense.

Anonymous

Don't buy the "special" without checking quality. The apple in that marked-down bag may be bruised. Don't buy food you don't need just because it's cheap. A bargain that turns spoiled is no bargain.

James A. Beard

Come . . . without money and without price. Why do you spend your money for that which is not bread?

The Bible

Who lives content with little possesses everything.

Nicolas Boileau-Despreaux

Prudence is no doubt a valuable quality, but prudence which degenerates into timidity is very seldom the path to safety.

Viscount Cecil

Shop alone if possible. You will be better able to concentrate, and other members of the family will not be adding unnecessary—and often expensive—items to the shopping cart.

The Redbook Cookbook

There is no dignity quite so impressive, and no independence quite so important as living within your means . . . Any other course for me would be as the senseless imitation of a fowl which was attempting to light higher than its roost.

Calvin Coolidge

When you go to buy, use your eyes, not your ears.

Czech proverb

You can't eat well and keep fit if you don't shop well.

Adelle Davis

Beware of little expenses; a small leak will sink a great ship.

Benjamin Franklin

Choose such pleasures as recreate and cost little.

Thomas Fuller

He will always be a slave who does not know how to live upon a little.

Horace

The real world is not easy to live in. It is rough; it is slippery. Without the most clear-eyed adjustments we fall and get crushed. A man must stay sober: not always, but most of the time.

Clarence Day

A full cup must be carried steadily.

English proverb

Be careful, and you will save many men from the sin of robbing you.

Edgar Watson Howe

All the money in the world is no use to a man or his country if he spends it as fast as he makes it. All he has left is his bills and the reputation for being a fool.

Rudyard Kipling

No gain is so certain as that which proceeds from the economical use of what you already have.

Latin proverb

How to improve goods and services? Learn to complain, politely and firmly, when you receive what you believe to be inferior goods or services. Don't register your complaint with the salesperson or the waiter, but with the boss or the owner. He'll listen.

Stanley Marcus

Money is never spent to so much advantage as when you have been cheated out of it: for at one stroke you have purchased prudence.

Schopenhauer

The art of living easily as to money is to pitch your scale of living one degree below your means.

Henry Taylor

We are not to judge thrift solely by the test of saving or spending. If one spends what he should prudently save, that certainly is to be deplored. But if one saves what he should prudently spend, that is not necessarily to be commended. A wise balance between the two is the desired end.

Owen D. Young

Open your mouth and purse cautiously, and your stock of wealth and reputation shall, at least in repute, be great.

Zimmerman

I live from hand to mouth, content to have enough for my ordinary expenses. As to extraordinary contingencies, not all the scrimping in the world would suffice.

Michel de Montaigne

The man who gets rich quickly must economize quickly, or he'll go hungry quickly.

Plautus

Q

Quality of Life

Quality of Life

Not every man wants to be a millionaire; many are content just to live like one.

Anonymous

If money is all that a man makes, then he will be poor—poor in happiness, poor in all that makes life worth living.

Herbert N. Casson

A greater poverty than that caused by lack of money is the poverty of unawareness. Men and women go about the world unaware of the beauty, the goodness, the glories in it. Their souls are poor. It is better to have a poor pocketbook than to suffer from a poor soul.

Thomas Dreier

Many a man would have been worse if his estate had been better.

Benjamin Franklin

Like Heav'n it hears the orphans' cries,
And wipes the tears from widows' eyes.

John Gay

One can accumulate enough wealth to buy a golden bed, but one cannot buy sound sleep with money.

Daniel Arap Moi

I'd rather have roses on my table than diamonds on my neck.

Emma Goldman

Who wait for dead men go long barefoot.

John Heywood

There are only two ways to be rich: have much, or be content with little.

Anonymous

It is better to live rich than to die rich.

Samuel Johnson

Neither locks had they to their doors nor bars to their windows;
But their dwellings were open as day and the hearts of the owners;
There the richest was poor and the poorest lived in abundance.

Henry Wadsworth Longfellow

I've never been poor, only broke. Being poor is a frame of mind. Being broke is only a temporary situation.

Mike Todd

Don't try to die rich but live rich.

Thomas Bird Mosher

What riches have you that you deem me poor,
Or what large comfort that you call me sad?

George Santayana

I have no riches but my thoughts,
Yet these are wealth enough for me.

Sara Teasdale

R

Racism
Religion
Reputation
Respect
Responsibility
Risk

Racism

Racism is the snobbery of the poor.

Raymond Aron

Let the Afro-American depend on no party, but on himself for his salvation. Let him continue to education, build character, and above all, put money in his purse. When he has a dollar in his pocket and many more in the bank, he can move from injustice and oppression and no one to say him nay. When he has money, and plenty of it, parties and races will become his servants.

Ida B. Wells

Religion

Render therefore unto Caesar the things which are Caesar's and unto God the things that are God's.

The Bible

Thy money perish with thee, because thou hast thought that the gift of God may be purchased with money.

The Bible

Trust in your money and down you go!
Trust in God and flourish as a tree.

The Bible

It is an anomaly of modern life that many find giving to be a burden. Such persons have omitted a preliminary giving. If one first gives himself to the Lord, all other giving is easy.

John S. Bonnell

You ought to have money. If you can honestly attain unto riches in Philadelphia, it is your Christian and godly duty to do so. It is an awful mistake of those pious people to think you must be awfully poor in order to be pious.

Russell H. Conwell

When it is a question of money, everybody is of the same religion.

Voltaire

Money is God in action.

Frederick J. Eikerenkoetter II
('Reverend Ike')

It is the perpetual tendency of wealth to draw on the spiritual class, not in this coarse way, but in plausible and covert ways.

Ralph Waldo Emerson

The sumptuously furnished house may be only an exquisitely sculptured tomb; the scantily furnished house may be the very hearth-stone of the eternal God.

John Henry Jowett

The greatest man in history was the poorest.

Ralph Waldo Emerson

The only money of God is God.

Ralph Waldo Emerson

Money is the wise man's religion.

Euripides

(Money is) the god of our time.

Heinrich Heine

We ought to change the legend on our money from "In God We Trust" to "In Money We Trust." Because, as a nation, we've got far more faith in money these days than we do in God.

Arthur Hope

Folks are serious about three things—their religion, their family, and most of all, their money.

Thomas Bertram Lance

Ye cannot serve God and Mammon. If ye love the one, ye will hate the other. Every proof that we love Mammon with all our heart and all our soul raises the presumption that we have lost the love of God and are merely going through the motions when we worship him.

Walter Rauschenbusch

The rich should tremble at the threatenings of Jesus Christ.

Pope Leo XIII

God is all-powerful, and money is his lieutenant.

Spanish proverb

Men's pennies and God's promises don't very well go together to buy heaven.

Charles Haddon Spurgeon

Remember that sore saying spoken once by Him that was the truth, "How hard it is for the rich man to enter into heaven!" Let all rich men remember that hard word.

Alfred Lord Tennyson

Nothing that is God's is obtainable by money.

Tertullian

Reputation

Wealth by which some people think to get a reputation does but expose the more their weaknesses and follies.

Anonymous

The world at large does not judge us by who we are and what we know; it judges us by what we have.

Joyce Brothers

(Wealth is) a good name.

Miguel de Cervantes

The rich are the scum of the earth in every country.

G.K. Chesterton

He that is of opinion money will do everything may well be suspected of doing everything for money.

Benjamin Franklin

Bad neighbors count a man's income, not his expenses.

Hebrew proverb

Wealth brings virtue and fame.

Hesiod

The most valuable of all human possessions, next to a superior and disdainful air, is the reputation of being well to do.

H. L. Mencken

Respectable means rich, and decent means poor. I should die if I heard my family called decent.

Thomas Love Peacock

It takes a strong man to be mean. A mean man is one that has the courage not to be generous. When I give a tip it is not because I want to but because I'm afraid of what the waiter will think. Russell Sage is one of Nature's noblemen.

Russell Sage

The best way to attract money, she had discovered, was to give the appearance of having it.

Gail Sheehy

No man is rich enough to buy back his past.

Oscar Wilde

Money sometimes makes fools of important persons, but it may also make important persons of fools.

Walter Winchell

Respect

As long as I am rich reputed,
With solemn voice I am saluted;
But wealth away once worn,
Not one will say good morn.

Anonymous

(Money is) an evidence of culture and a passbook into polite society.

Anonymous

In civilized society, external advantages make us more respected. A man with a good coat upon his back meets with a better reception than he who has a bad one.

James Boswell

Money is honey, my little sonny,
And a rich man's joke is always funny.

Thomas Edward Brown

Wealth per se I never too much valued, and my acquaintance with its possessors has by no means increased my veneration for it.

Francis Burney

Whoso has sixpence is sovereign (to the length of sixpence) over all men; commands cooks to feed him, philosophers to teach him, kings to mount guard over him,—to the length of sixpence.

Thomas Carlyle

My money doth make me full merry to be,
And without my money none careth for me.

Thomas Deloney

Do not trust all men, but trust men of worth; the former course is silly, the latter a mark of prudence.

Democritus

Money and goods are certainly the best of references.

Charles Dickens

No matter what you do, you can't dishonour yourself when you are rich.

Denis Diderot

Once you are rich you will find yourself very highly esteemed.

Giambattista Cinthio Giraldi

Wealth excuses folly.

Horace

Go into the street, and give one man a lecture on morality, and another a shilling and see which will respect you most.

Samuel Johnson

Deceive the rich and powerful if you will, but don't insult them.

Japanese proverb

With money in your pocket, you are wise, and you are handsome, and you sing well too.

Jewish proverb

According to the amount of money a man has in his coffers, so is he respected.

Juvenal

There is more safety in men's good opinion than in money.

Latin proverb

I don't say he's a great man. Willy Loman never made a lot of money. His name was never in the paper. He's not the finest character that ever lived. But he's a human being, and a terrible thing is happening to him. So attention must be paid. He's not to be allowed to fall into his grave like an old dog. Attention, attention must be finally paid to such a person.

Arthur Miller (Playwright)
Death of a Salesman (Play)

I do not dislike but I certainly have no especial respect or admiration for and no trust in, the typical big moneyed men of my country. I do not regard them as furnishing sound opinion as respects either foreign or domestic business.

Theodore Roosevelt

When I had money everyone called me brother.

Polish proverb

The man who damns money has obtained it dishonorably; the man who respects it has earned it.

Ayn Rand

The rich man is everywhere expected and at home.

Sa'Di

Let all the learn'd say what they can,
'Tis ready money makes the man;
Commands respect wher'er we go,
And gives a grace to all we do.

William Somerville

Make money and the whole world will conspire to call you a gentleman.

Mark Twain

Responsibility

Live within your income, even if you have to borrow to do so.

Josh Billings

He is rich enough that needeth neither to flatter nor to borrow.

Thomas Fuller

If thou wouldst keep money, save money;
If thou wouldst reap money, sow money.

Thomas Fuller

If a man has money, it is usually a sign too, that he knows how to take care of it; don't imagine his money is easy to get simply because he has plenty of it.

Ed Howe

A man is led the way he wishes to follow.

Huna

The buck stops with the guy who signs the checks.

Rupert Murdoch

Wealth lightens not the hearts and cares of men.

Tibullus

With all its alluring promise that some one else will guarantee for the rainy day, social security can never replace the program that man's future welfare is, after all, a matter of individual responsibility.

Harold Stonier

I am firm in my belief that anyone not only can be rich but ought to be rich.

John J. Raskob

Many wealthy people are little more than the janitors of their possessions.

Frank Lloyd Wright

Risk

Be not penny-wise; riches have wings; sometimes they fly away of themselves, and sometimes they must be set flying to bring in more.

Francis Bacon

To get profit without risk, experience without danger, and reward without work, is as impossible as it is to live without being born.

A.P. Gouthev

Take calculated risks. That is quite different from being rash.

George S. Patton

S

Saving, Savings

When saving for old age, be sure to put away a few pleasant thoughts.

Anonymous

Any young man with good health and a poor appetite can save up money.

James Montgomery Bailey

Men who make money rarely saunter; men who save money rarely swagger.

Edward G. E. Bulwer-Lytton

There is nothing in saving money. The thing to do with it is to put it back into yourself, into your work, into the thing that is important, into whatever you are so much interested in that it is more important than money.

Henry Ford

You seem to think that everyone can save money if they have the character to do it. As a matter of fact, there are innumerable people who have a wide choice between saving and giving their children the best possible opportunities. The decision is usually in favor of the children.

Eleanor Roosevelt

When one has had to work so hard to get money, why should he impose himself the further hardship of trying to save it?

Don Herold

The habit of saving is itself an education; it fosters every virtue, teaches self-denial, cultivates the sense of order, trains to forethought, and so broadens the mind.

T. T. Munger

You may not have saved a lot of money in your life, but if you have saved a lot of heartaches for other folks, you are a pretty rich man.

Seth Parker

There is a certain Buddhistic calm that comes from having . . . money in the bank.

Tom Robbins

Service

To give real service you must add something which cannot be bought or measured with money, and that is sincerity and integrity.

Donald A. Adams

He who does kind deeds becomes rich.

Hindu proverb

I expect to pass through this world but once. Any good therefore that I can do, or any kindness that I can show to any fellow creature let me do it now. Let me not defer or neglect it, for I shall not pass this way again.

Stephen Grellet

If you are poor, distinguish yourself by your virtues; if rich, by your good deeds.

Joseph Joubert

Sex

Money, it turned out, was exactly like sex; you thought of nothing else if you didn't have it and thought of other things if you did.

James Baldwin

The big difference between sex for money and sex for free is that sex for money usually costs a lot less.

Brendan Francis

Without money we do not have to pretend with prudent women, for affairs are worthless without it.

Tirso de Molina

Whether he admits it or not, a man has been brought up to look at money as a sign of his virility, a symbol of his power, a bigger phallic symbol than a Porsche.

Victoria Billings

It is not human "to act the beast," to deify sexuality and set it up as an absolute. Raw sexual appetite is no more a sign of love than violence and brutality are signs of strength.

Henri Gibert

About money and sex it is impossible to be truthful ever; one's ego is too involved.

Malcolm Muggeridge

Money and sex are forces too unruly for our reason; they can only be controlled by taboos which we tamper with at our peril.

Logan Pearsall Smith

Socialism

A liberal is a man who is willing to spend somebody else's money.

Carter Glass

Wells and Shaw are the best known Socialist leaders among people who write English. But they are different from the Socialists I knew in the hot days of my youth . . . They belong to what might be called the Take-It-Aisy School of Socialism. They are opposed to Capitalism but not to Capital, when it adopts the form of a tidy balance in their own name at Barclay's Bank.

Finley Peter Dunne

Communism is a hateful thing . . . But the communism of combined wealth and capital . . . is not less dangerous than the communism of oppressed poverty and toil.

Grover Cleveland

Sources

(Riches are) a gift from God.

Jehiel Anav

Know from the bounteous heavens all riches flow;
And what man gives, the gods by man bestow.

Homer

Money smells good no matter what its source.

Latin proverb

Speculation

Don't speculate unless you can make it a full-time job. Beware of barbers, beauticians, waiters—of anyone—bringing gifts of "inside" information or "tips" . . . Don't try to buy at the bottom and sell at the top. This can't be done—except by liars.

Bernard M. Baruch

An economist is an expert who will know tomorrow why the things he predicted yesterday didn't happen today.

Laurence J. Peter

(Money is) an eel in the hand.

Welsh proverb

There are two times in a man's life when he should not speculate: when he can't afford it and when he can.

Mark Twain

Spending

A tightwad may be a great success in making money, but is a terrible failure in spending it.

Anonymous

Spare when you are young and spend when you are old.

H.G. Bohn

I've never been a big spender. Certainly not in my personal life—as my friends will attest—and not in the public offices I have held. I am not a fiscal conservative. I'm just cheap.

Jerry Brown

Riches are for spending, and spending for honour and good actions.

Francis Bacon

We don't want a thing because we have found a reason for it; we find a reason for it because we want it.

Will Durant

My neighbor, a jolly farmer, in the tavern bar-room, thinks that the use of money is sure and speedy spending. For his part, he says, he puts his down his neck and gets the good of it.

Ralph Waldo Emerson

Get to know two things about a man—how he earns his money and how he spends it—and you have the clue to his character, for you have a searchlight that shows up the inmost recesses of his soul.

Robert James McCracken

A man's treatment of money is the most decisive test of his character—how he makes it and how he spends it.

James Moffatt

Money would be more enjoyable if it took people as long to spend it as it does to earn it.

Ed Howe

Never buy what you do not want, because it is cheap; it will be dear to you.

Thomas Jefferson

I am dying, as I have lived, beyond my means.

Oscar Wilde

A little wanton money . . . burned out the bottom of his purse.

Thomas More

O money, money, money! I often stop to wonder how thou canst go out so fast when thou comest in so slowly.

Ogden Nash

Expenditure rises to meet income.

C. Northcote Parkinson

Though I am much against too much spending, yet I do think it best to enjoy some degree of pleasure now that we have health, money, and opportunity, rather than to leave pleasures to old age and poverty, when we cannot have them so properly.

Samuel Pepys

The lawful basis of wealth is, that a man who works should be paid the fair value of his work, and that if he does not choose to spend it today, he should have free leave to keep it, and spend it tomorrow.

John Ruskin

Economy is half the battle of life; it is not so hard to earn money as to spend it well.

Charles Haddon Spurgeon

Almost any man knows how to earn money, but not one in a million knows how to spend it. If he had known so much as this, he would never have earned it.

Thoreau

A newspaper reported that I spend $30,000 a year buying Paris clothes and that women hate me for it. I couldn't spend that much unless I wore sable underwear.

Jacqueline Kennedy Onassis

Stock Market

A man is robbed on the Stock Exchange, just as he is killed in a war, by people whom he never sees.

Alfred Capus

One of the funny things about the stock market is that every time one man buys, another sells, and both think they are astute.

William Feather

There is nothing like the ticker tape except a woman—nothing that promises, hour after hour, day after day, such sudden developments: nothing that disappoints so often or occasionally fulfills with such unbelievable passionate magnificence.

Walter Knowleton Gutman

Anyone who thinks there's safety in numbers hasn't looked at the stock market pages.

Irene Peter

Success

Money itself isn't the primary factor in what one does. A person does things for the sake of accomplishing something. Money generally follows.

Henry Crown

If you want your name to live after you, you'll not give all your thought to money. But, whether you want to make money, or write a book, or build a bridge, or run a streetcar—or do anything else successfully—you'll do well to remember that in all the world there is no word more important than—"Think!"

Edwin Baird

The jests of the rich are ever successful.

Oliver Goldsmith

Money is a dream. It is a piece of paper on which is imprinted in invisible ink the dream of all the things it will buy, all the trinkets and all the power over others. A kind of institutionalized dream which, along with its companion dream-institution of Success, constitutes the main fantasy on which our way of life has been built.

David T. Bazelon

Success breeds success, just as money breeds money.

S. R. N. Chamfort

What's money? A man is a success if he gets up in the morning and gets to bed at night and in between he does what he wants to.

Bob Dylan

One of the best ways to ensure success is to develop expensive tastes, or marry someone who has them. The range of options open to those who succeed is so large as to encompass almost everything: yachts, art, clothes, jewelry, travel—all these can be yours.

Michael Korda

The success of some men in acquiring money is due to the success of other men in letting go of it.

Anonymous

Financial success improves people who are good and debases people who are bad.

John Osborne

Wealth does not bring excellence, but that wealth comes from excellence.

Plato

The two leading recipes for success are building a better mousetrap or finding a bigger loophole.

Edgar A. Shoaff

I do want to get rich but I never want to do what there is to do to get rich.

Gertrude Stein

I saw that a humble man, with the blessing of the Lord, might live on a little; and that where the heart was set on greatness, success in business did not satisfy the craving; but that commonly, with an increase of wealth, the desire of wealth is increased.

John Woolman

Money is a stupid measure of achievement but unfortunately it is the only universal measure we have.

Charles P. Steinmetz

Sufficiency

The best condition in life is not to be so rich as to be envied, nor so poor as to be damned.

Josh Billings

My riches consist not in the extent of my possessions but in the fewness of my wants.

J. Brotherton

Possessions, outward success, publicity, luxury—to me these have always been contemptible. I believe that a simple and unassuming manner of life is best for every one, best both for the body and the mind.

Albert Einstein

I have enough money to get by. I'm not independently wealthy, just independently lazy, I suppose.

Montgomery Clift

My problem lies in reconciling my gross habits with my net income.

Errol Flynn

He who curbs his desires will always be rich enough.

French proverb

He is rich enough that needeth neither to flatter nor to borrow.

Thomas Fuller

Moderate riches will carry you; if you have more, you must carry them.

Thomas Fuller

I am indeed rich, since my income is superior to my expense, and my expense is equal to my wishes.

Edward Gibbon

Wealth is not of necessity a curse, nor poverty a blessing. Wholesome and easy abundance is better than either; better for our manhood that we have enough for daily comfort; enough for culture, for hospitality, for Christian charity. More than this may or may not be a blessing. Certainly it can be a blessing only by being accepted as a trust.

Raymond Hitchcock

Better a steady dime than a rare dollar.

Hebrew proverb

We don't want to fight, but, by jingo, if we do, we've got the ships, we've got the men, we've got the money too.

G. W. Hunt

Be contented, when you have got all you want.

Holbrook Jackson

Want and wealth equally harden the human heart, as frost and fire are both alien to the human flesh. Famine and gluttony alike drive away nature from the heart of man.

Theodore E. Parker

It is not the man who has too little who is poor, but the one who hankers after more. What difference does it make how much there is laid away in a man's safe or in his barns, how many head of stock he grazes or how much capital he puts out at interest, if he is always after what is another's and only counts what he has yet to get, never what he has already. You ask what is the proper limit to a person's wealth? First, having what is essential, and second, having what is enough.

Seneca

Who is really rich? The man who is satisfied with his share.

Sayings of the Fathers

It is better to have old secondhand diamonds than none at all.

Mark Twain

He gave me half of his paycheck after taxes and felt that should be fine. Well, that only turned out to be $1,400 a month. I've got extravagant tastes for beautiful things, so that hardly paid for the children's Lacoste T-shirts.

Margaret Trudeau

It feels uncommonly queer to have enough cash to pay one's bills. I'd have sold my soul for it a few years ago!

Edith Wharton

Superficiality

Nothing is more fallacious than wealth. Today it is for thee, tomorrow it is against thee. It arms the eyes of the envious everywhere. It is a hostile comrade, a domestic enemy.

John Chrysostom

I don't think chic has anything to do with money. You can have all the money in the world and have no idea what elegance means.

Bianca Jagger

Hollywood money isn't money. It's congealed snow, melts in your hand, and there you are.

Dorothy Parker

Surplus Money

Save a part of your income and begin now, for the man with a surplus controls circumstances and the man without a surplus is controlled by circumstances.

Henry H. Buckley

Surplus wealth is a sacred trust which its possessor is bound to administer in his lifetime for the good of the community.

Andrew Carnegie

The men of greatest usefulness are those who have a surplus; those who have only good will and love for their fellows cannot equal in well-doing those who have money and success to their credit.

Ed Howe

The surplus wealth we have gained to some extent at least belongs to our fellow beings; we are only the temporary custodians of our fortunes, and let us be careful that no just complaint can be made against our stewardship.

Jacob H. Schiff

Superfluous wealth can buy superfluities only.

Thoreau

Never steal more than you actually need, for the possession of surplus money leads to extravagance, foppish attire, frivolous thought.

Dalton Trumbo

T

Taxes

Thrift

Time

Taxes

Count the day won when, turning on its axis,
This world imposes no additional taxes.

Franklin P. Adams

An income tax form is like a laundry list—either way you lose your shirt.

Fred Allen

Money isn't everything; in fact, after the tax collector gets through, money isn't anything.

Anonymous

Taxes are going up so fast that government is likely to price itself right out of the market.

Dan Bennett

Why does a slight tax increase cost you two hundred dollars and a substantial tax cut save you thirty cents?

Peg Bracken

Collecting more taxes than is absolutely necessary is legalized robbery.

Calvin Coolidge

The only thing that hurts more than paying an income tax is not having to pay an income tax.

Thomas R. Duwar

The hardest thing in the world to understand is the income tax.

Albert Einstein

The reward of energy, enterprise and thrift—is taxes.

William Feather

As fast as we cut our expenses, the government raises our taxes.

William Feather

I'm proud to be paying taxes in the United Staes. The only thing is—I could be just as proud for half the money.

Arthur Godfrey

I would suggest the taxation of all property equally whether church or corporation.

Ulysses S. Grant

Bing (Crosby) doesn't pay an income tax anymore. He just asks the government what they need.

Bob Hope

Anybody has a right to evade taxes if he can get away with it. No citizen has a moral obligation to assist in maintaining the government.

J. P. Morgan

Capital punishment: The income tax.

Jeff Hayes

The avoidance of taxes is the only intellectual pursuit that still carries any reward.

John Maynard Keynes

Tax reform means, "Don't tax you, don't tax me.
Tax that fellow behind the tree."

Russell Long

The trouble with being a breadwinner nowadays is that the government is in for such a big slice.

Mary McCoy

We owe it to our country to pay our taxes without murmuring; the time to get in our fine work is on the valuation.

Edgar Wilson Nye

In levying taxes and in shearing sheep it is well to stop when you get down to the skin.

Austin O'Malley

The taxpayer—that's someone who works for the federal government but doesn't have to take a civil service examination.

Ronald Reagan

People want just taxes more than they want lower taxes. They want to know that every man is paying his proportionate share according to his wealth.

Will Rogers

The income tax has made more liars out of the American people than golf has. Even when you make a tax form out on the level, you don't know when it's through if you are a crook or a martyr.

Will Rogers

Nothing makes a man and wife feel closer, these days, than a joint tax return.

Gil Stern

There is just one thing I can promise you about the outer-space program: your tax dollar will go further.

Wernher von Braun

Thrift

Men are divided between those who are as thrifty as if they would live forever, and those who are as extravagant as if they were going to die the next day.

Aristotle

Thrift and prosperity have gone hand in hand since Abraham's flocks grew and multiplied. Thrift is not, as many suppose, a self-repression. It is self-expression, the demonstration of a will and ability to raise one's self to a higher plane of living. No depression was ever caused by people having too much money in reserve. No human being ever became a social drifter through the practice of sensible thrift.

Harvey A. Blodgett

So often we rob tomorrow's memories by today's economies.

John Mason Brown

The world abhors closeness, and all but admires extravagance; yet a slack hand shows weakness, and a tight hand strength.

Thomas Buxton

Economy is in itself a source of great revenue.

Seneca

Thrift is that habit of character that prompts one to work for what he gets, to earn what is paid him; to invest a part of his earnings; to spend wisely and well; to save, but not hoard.

Arthur Chamberlain

The thriftiest with money are the most spendthrift with desires.

Moses Ibn Ezra, Shirat Yisrael

If a man should discover a treasure, he would be the richer, but not necessarily more thrifty.

Greek proverb

(Money is) saint-seducing gold.

Shakespeare

The doctrine of thrift for the poor is dumb and cruel, like advising them to try and lift themselves by their bootstraps.

Norman Thomas

Time

Possessions dwindle: I mourn their loss. But I mourn the loss of time much more; for anyone can save his purse, but none can win back lost time.

Latin proverb

When told of a man who had acquired great wealth, a sage replied, "Has he also acquired the days in which to spend it?"

Ibn Gabirol

Money never cometh out of season.

Thomas Drake

Time is really the only capital that any human being has, and the one thing that he can't afford to lose.

Thomas Edison

Money and time are the heaviest burden of life, and the unhappiest of all mortals are those who have more of either than they know how to use. To set himself free from these incumbrances, one hurries to Newmarket; another travels over Europe; one pulls down his house and calls architects about him; another buys a seat in the country, and follows his hounds over hedges and through rivers; one makes collections of shells; and another searches the world for tulips and carnations.

Samuel Johnson

(Our riches are) that which gives us time.

Adapted from Charles Lamb

Money is time. With money I buy for cheerful use the hours which otherwise would not in any sense be mine; nay, which would make me their miserable bondsman.

George Gissing

U

Upward Mobility
Utilization

Upward Mobility

Some people want champagne and caviar when they should have beer and hot dogs.

Dwight D. Eisenhower

Improvement of one's economic position is helped more by cool persistence than by hot enthusiasm.

William Feather

The gaps (between rich and poor) aren't bad. They create a kind of void which exerts an upward situation. It's like the successive waves of immigrants in the United States and their changing upward economic roles. On a worldwide basis, this happens in much more complex ways but, in some ways, even more rapidly.

Herman Kahn

Utilization

More people should learn to tell their dollars where to go instead of asking them where they went.

Roger Babson

If you ever have a lump of money large enough to be of any use, and can spare it, don't give it away: find some needed job that nobody is doing and get it done.

George Bernard Shaw

Seek not proud riches, but rather such as thou mayest get justly, use soberly, distribute cheerfully, and leave contentedly.

Francis Bacon

Be not penny-wise; riches have wings, and sometimes they fly away of themselves, sometimes they must be set flying to bring in more.

Francis Bacon

Making money is fun, but it's pointless if you don't use the power it brings.

John Bentley

Riches do not consist in the possession of treasures, but in the use made of them.

Napoleon Bonaparte

Without doubt, the highest privilege of wealth is the opportunity it affords for doing good, without giving up one's fortune.

Cicero

All the good things of the world are no further good to us than they are of use; and of all we may heap up we enjoy only as much as we can use, and no more.

Daniel DeFoe

If a rich man is proud of his wealth, he should not be praised until it is known how he employs it.

Socrates

Money is like an arm or a leg—use it or lose it.

Henry Ford

The highest use of capital is not to make more money, but to make money do more for the betterment of life.

Henry Ford

The use of money is all the advantage there is in having money.

Benjamin Franklin

Capital as such is not evil; it is its wrong use that is evil.

Mohandas Gandhi

It is one thing to have a right to the possession of money, and another to have a right to use money as one pleases.

Pope Leo XIII

Undermine the entire structure of society by leaving the pay toilet door ajar so the next person can get in free.

Taylor Mead

Blessed is the man who has both mind and money, for he employs the latter well.

Menander

You are wealthy. And what is the end of it? When you depart, do you trail your riches after you as you are being pulled to your tomb? You gather wealth by spending time, but you cannot pile up a heavier measure of life.

Palladas

Be rather bountiful than expensive; do good with what thou hast, or it will do thee no good.

William Penn

By doing good with his money, a man, as it were, stamps the image of God upon it, and makes it pass current for the merchandise of heaven.

J. Rutledge

A gentleman of our days is one who has money enough to do what every fool would do if he could afford it: that is, consume without producing.

George Bernard Shaw

I was born unto it and there was nothing I could do about it. It was there, like air or food or any other element . . .The only question with wealth is what you do with it.

John D. Rockefeller, Jr.

It is not a custom with me to keep money to look at it.

George Washington

Finance is the art of passing currency from hand to hand until it finally disappears.

Robert W. Sarnoff

Money alone is only a mean; it presupposes a man to use it. The rich man can go where he pleases, but perhaps please himself nowhere. He can buy a library or visit the whole world, but perhaps has neither patience to read nor intelligence to see . . . The purse may be full and the heart empty. He may have gained the world and lost himself; and with all his wealth around him . . . he may live as blank a life as any tattered ditcher.

Robert Louis Stevenson

To get money you must spend it.

Plautus

V

Value

Virtue

Value

(The dollar is) a friend that opens doors.

Anonymous

Thy money perish with thee.

The Bible

Money: a blessing that is of no advantage to us excepting when we part with it.

Ambrose Bierce

In its famous paradox, the equation of money and excrement, psychoanalysis becomes the first science to state what common sense and the poets have long known—that the essence of money is in its absolute worthlessness.

Norman O. Brown

After all, money, as they say, is miraculous.

Thomas Carlyle

Even the blind can see money.

Chinese proverb

Money, which represents the prose of life, and which is hardly spoken of in parlors without an apology, is in its effects and laws, as beautiful as roses.

Ralph Waldo Emerson

One bag of money is stronger than two bags of truth.

Danish proverb

Money is a fruit that is always ripe.

English proverb

Things are never as good with money as they are bad without it.

Hebrew proverb

To learn the value of money, it is not necessary to know the nice things it can get for you, you have to have experienced the trouble of getting it.

Philippe Heriat

(The dollar is) a sacred . . . object, contact with which is looked upon as curative and prophylactic.

Elbert Hubbard

Surely there comes a time when counting the cost and paying the price aren't things to think about anymore. All that matters is value—the ultimate value of what one does.

James Hilton

Wealth is nothing in itself, it is not useful but when it departs from us; its value is found only in that which it can purchase, which, if we suppose it put to its best use by those that possess it, seems not much to deserve the desire or envy of a wise man. It is certain that, with regard to corporal enjoyment, money can neither open new avenues to pleasure, nor block up the passages of anguish. Disease and infirmity still continue to torture and enfeeble, perhaps exasperated by luxury, or promoted by softness. With respect to the mind, it has rarely been observed, that wealth contributes much to quicken the discernment, enlarge the capacity, or elevate the imagination; but may, by hiring flattery, or laying diligence asleep, confirm error, and harden stupidity.

Samuel Johnson

I was not corrupt. Perhaps that is the only thing I regret. I've realized, after fourteen months in this country, the value of money, whether it is clean or dirty.

Nguyen Cao Ky

The dollar has become like a hydrant at an international convention of dogs.

Eliot Janeway

The value of money is that with it we can tell any man to go to the devil. It is the sixth sense which enables you to enjoy the other five.

William Sommerset Maugham

Let him live in his poverty and not sin.
For money is a sterile thing.

Martin Luther

The chief value of money lies in the fact that one lives in a world in which it is overestimated.

H. L. Mencken

Money cannot buy peace of mind, greatness of spirit, serenity, confidence, or self-sufficiency.

Plutarch

A penny is something we see every day but never look at.

Stephen Potter

(Wealth is) life.

John Ruskin

Who steals my purse steals trash.

Shakespeare

Riches get their value from the mind of their possessor; they are blessings to those who know how to use them, curse to those who do not.

Terence

No objects of value . . . are worth risking the priceless experience of waking up one more day.

Jack Smith

Money is what it will buy.

Spanish proverb

Dollars cannot buy yesterday.

Harold R. Stark

Most of the luxuries, and many of the so-called comforts of life, are not only not indispensable, but positive hindraces to the elevation of mankind. With respect to luxuries and comforts, the wisest have ever lived a more simple and meager life than the poor.

Thoreau

Of a life of luxury the fruit is luxury, whether in agriculture, or commerce, or literature, or art. There are nowadays professors of philosophy, but not philosophers. Yet it is admirable to profess because it was once admirable to live.

Thoreau

Money is the means by which you can purchase everything but happiness and health, and will pay your ticket to all places but Heaven.

Clinton Wallace

Virtue

I cannot call Riches better than the baggage of virtue. The Roman word is better, impedimenta. For the baggage is to an army, so is riches to virtue. It cannot be spared nor left behind, but it hindereth the march; yea and the care of it sometimes loseth or disturbeth the victory.

Francis Bacon

Prosperity doth best discover vice; but adversity doth best discover virtue.

Francis Bacon

No man can tell whether he is rich or poor by turning to his ledger. It is the heart that makes a man rich. He is rich according to what he is, not according to what he has.

Henry Ward Beecher

You must put your hand into a man's heart to find out how much he is worth, not into his pocket.

Henry Ward Beecher

It is better to have little and be godly than to own an evil man's wealth.

The Bible

What is a man profited, if he shall gain the whole world, and lose his own soul?

The Bible

Your riches won't help you on Judgment Day; only righteousness counts then.

The Bible

Without a rich heart, wealth is an ugly beggar.

Ralph Waldo Emerson

He who is plenteously provided for from within needs but little from without.

Johann W. von Goethe

First secure an independent income, then practice virtue.

Greek proverb

A man is usually more careful of his money than he is of his principles.

Ed Howe

Give unto the orphans their property, and give them not the vile in exchange for the good, and devour not their property to your own property; verily, that were a great sin.

The Koran

One of the advantages of being poor is that it necessitates the cultivation of the virtues.

Jerome K. Jerome

God takes notice of clean hands, not full hands.

Latin proverb

Money has become the grand test of virtue.

George Orwell

The wise and moral man
Shines like a fire on a hill top,
Making money like the bee,
Who does not hurt the flower.

The Pali Canon

There is no sound basis upon which it may be assumed that all poor men are godly and all rich men are evil, no more than it could be assumed that all rich men are good and all poor men are bad.

Norman Vincent Peale

Goodness does not come from possessions . . . goodness alone makes possessions or anything else worth having, whether in public or in private life.

Socrates

If I keep my good character, I shall be rich enough.

Platonicus

The glory that goes with wealth and beauty is fleeting and fragile; virtue is a possession glorious and eternal.

Sallust

We all ask whether he is wealthy; none whether he is good.

Seneca

Fortune can rob me of my wealth, but not my soul.

Seneca

Are you not ashamed of heaping up the greatest amount of money and honour and reputation, and caring so little about wisdom and truth and the greatest improvement of the soul.

Socrates

The primary and sole foundation of virtue or of the proper conduct of life is to seek our own profit.

Spinoza

W

War
Waste
Wealth, Corporate
Wealth, Personal
Wisdom
Women
Work

War

Where there is money, there is fighting.

Marian Anderson

The sinews of art and literature, like those of war, are money.

Samuel Butler

(Money) The sinews of war.

Cicero

Peace makes money and money makes war.

French proverb

When the rich make war, it's the poor who die.

Jean-Paul Sartre

Waste

Nature is the most thrifty thing in the world; she never wastes anything; she undergoes change, but there's no annihilation—the essence remains.

T. Binney

The man who tips a shilling every time he stops for petrol is giving away annually the cost of lubricating his car.

J. Paul Getty

Up and down the City Road, in and out the Eagle,
That's the way the money goes—pop goes the weasel!

W.R. Mondale

Benjamin Franklin went through life an altered man because he once paid too dearly for a penny whistle. My concern springs usually from a deeper source, to wit, from having bought a whistle when I did not want one.

Robert Louis Stevenson

Wealth, Corporate

Capital formation is shifting from the entrepreneur who invests in the future to the pension trustee who invests in the past.

Peter Drucker

We must have a political state powerful enough to deal with corporate wealth, but how are we going to keep that state with its augmenting power from being captured by the force we want it to control?

Vernon Louis Parrington

The true friend of the people should see that they be not too poor, for extreme poverty lowers the character of the democracy; measures therefore should be taken which will give them lasting prosperity; and as this is equally the interest of all classes, the proceeds of the public revenues should be accumulated and distributed among its poor, if possible, in such quantities as may enable them to purchase a little farm, or, at any rate, make a beginning in trade or husbandry.

Aristotle

Humans must breathe, but corporations must make money.

Alice Embree

The money power preys upon the Nation in times of peace and conspires against it in times of adversity. It is more despotic than monarchy, more insolent than autocracy, more selfish than bureaucracy. It denounces, as public enemies, all who question its methods, or throw light upon its crimes.

William Jennings Bryan

We can have democracy in this country or we can have great wealth concentrated in the hands of a few, but we can't have both.

Louis D. Brandeis

When wealth is centralized the people are dispersed; when wealth is distributed the people are brought together.

Confucius

Nobody, but nobody, has to be poor in this country. If I wasn't making movies, I could go out in the street and make $500 a week selling pencils.

James Caan

If our economy of freedom fails to distribute wealth as ably as it has created it, the road to dictatorship will be open to any man who can persuasively promise security to all.

Willard Ariel Durant

Whoever controls the volume of money in any country is absolute master of all industry and commerce.

James A. Garfield

Ill fares the land, to hastening ills a prey,
Where wealth accumulates and men decay.

Oliver Goldsmith

The more affluent a society is, the more pronounced is the sense of ultimate emptiness and alienation on the part of its members.

Billy Graham

The Irish famine of 1846 killed more than a million people, but it killed poor devils only. To the wealth of the country it did not the slightest damage.

Karl Marx

I take for granted Jefferson's dictum that money, not morality, constitutes the principle of commercial nations.

Lewis H. Lapham

Blessed are the young, for they shall inherit the national debt.

Herbert Hoover

Those who own the country ought to govern it.

John Jay

A decent provision for the poor is the true test of civilization.

Samuel Johnson

If a free society cannot help the many who are poor, it cannot save the few who are rich.

John F. Kennedy

Every stable government in history has depended on the resignation of the poor to being poor.

Felicite de Lamennais

Capitalism . . . is outrageously unjust; it requires a continuing maldistribution of wealth in order to exist . . . We live in the twilight of an epoch . . . I am absolutely convinced that we are moving toward some kind of planned economy.

Michael Harrington

When the nation is poor, private poverty springs from the general calamity, and is, if I may so express myself, the general calamity itself. All the hospitals in the world cannot cure this private poverty; on the contrary, the spirit of indolence, which it constantly inspires, increases the general, and consequently the private, misery.

Montesquieu

In a country where there are no rich there will be only the poor—the very poor.

Walter Rathenau

There is no wealth but life. That country is the richest which nourishes the greatest number of noble and happy human beings; that man is richest who, having perfected the functions of his own life to the utmost, has also the widest helpful influence, both personal, and by means of his possessions, over the lives of others.

John Ruskin

The crying need of the nation is not for better morals, cheaper bread, temperance, liberty, culture, redemption of fallen sisters and erring brothers, nor the grace, love and fellowship of the Trinity, but simply for enough money.

George Bernard Shaw

The United States spends less proportionately on social welfare than almost any other industrial country.

Time magazine

The liberal reward of labour . . . as it is the necessary effect, so it is the natural symptom of increasing national wealth. The scanty maintenance of the labouring poor, on the other hand, is the natural symptom that things are at a stand, and their starving condition that they are going fast backwards.

Adam Smith

To assist every one who is needy far surpasses the strength or profit of a private person, for the wealth of a private person is altogether insufficient to supply such wants. Besides, the power of any one man is too limited for him to be able to unite every one with himself in friendship. The care, therefore, of the poor is incumbent on the whole of society and concerns only the general profit.

Spinoza

Some persons of a desponding spirit are in great concern about that vast number of poor people who are aged, diseased, or maimed, and I have been desired to employ my thoughts on what course may be taken to ease the nation of so grievous an encumbrance. But I am not in the least pain upon that matter, because it is very well known that they are every day dying, and rotting, by cold and famine, and filth, and vermin, as fast as you can be reasonably expected.

Jonathon Swift

Money is indeed the most important thing in the world; and all sound and successful personal and national morality should have this fact for its basis.

George Bernard Shaw

Wealth, Personal

Money isn't everything, but subtract it from some people and there's nothing left.

Anonymous

If a fool and his money are soon parted, why are there so many rich fools?

Anonymous

A little house filled, a little land well tilled, and a little wife well willed, are great riches.

Anonymous

(Wealth is) a matter of personal outlook.

Anonymous

There's no money in poetry, but then there's no poetry in money either.

Robert Graves

One of the main things money provides is privacy.

Paul Mellon

He had so much money that he could afford to look poor.

Edgar Wallace

At this time my farm gave me and my whole family a good living on the produce of it, and left me one year with another one hundred and fifty silver dollars, for I never spent more than ten dollars a year, which was for salt, nails, and the like. Nothing to eat, drink or wear was bought, as my farm provided all.

Anonymous

If you would know what the Lord God thinks of money, you have only to look at those to whom he gives it.

Maurice Baring

I was lucky. When God rained manna from heaven, I had a spoon.

Peter Drucker

It is rude and inconsiderate to overtip. It only makes things difficult—and embarrassing—for people who are not as rich as I am.

J. Paul Getty

When a man says money can do anything, that settles it—he hasn't any.

Ed Howe

We all covet wealth, but not its perils.

Jean de La Bruyère

The only incurable troubles of the rich are the troubles that money can't cure. Which is a kind of trouble which is even more troublesome if you are poor.

Ogden Nash

It doesn't matter if you're rich or poor, as long as you've got money.

Joe E. Lewis

Wealth is any income that is at least one hundred dollars more a year than the income of one's wife's sister's husband.

H.L. Mencken

It is good for a man to have that wherewith he may live well and happily.

Henry More

God shows his contempt for wealth by the kind of person he selects to receive it.

Austin O'Malley

Those who condemn wealth are those who have none and see no chance of getting it.

William Penn Patrick

They who know all the wealth they have, are poor; He's only rich that cannot tell his store.

John Suckling

(Wealth is) evidence of greatness.

Thomas B. Reed

(Wealth is) the possession of the valuable by the valiant.

John Ruskin

Reports of wealth or worth are best halved—and then halved again.

Spanish proverb

I've been rich and I've been poor; rich is better.

Sophie Tucker

The true perfection of man lies not in what man has, but in what man is.

Oscar Wilde

There is nothing more demoralizing than a small but adequate income.

Edmund Wilson

Wisdom

The best things in life are free, but it costs a lot of time and money before you find this out.

Anonymous

(Wealth is) the greatest force for good when spent wisely.

Anonymous

Silly people think that money commands the bodily goods most worth living.

Saint Thomas Aquinas

The price of wisdom is above rubies.

The Bible

What use is money in the hands of a stupid man?
Can he buy wisdom if he has no sense?

The Bible

Better have wisdom behind you than money.

The Bible

The foolish sayings of the rich pass for wise saws in society.

Miguel de Cervantes

If a man is wise, he gets rich, and if he gets rich, he gets foolish, or his wife does. That's what keeps the money movin' around.

Finley Peter Dunne

It is a common observation that any fool can get money; but they are not wise that think so.

Charles Caleb Colton

He that's rich is wise.

Daniel Defoe

The wisest man is the likeliest to possess all worldly blessings in an eminent degree; for as that moderation which wisdom prescribes is the surest way to useful wealth, so can it alone qualify us to taste many pleasures. The wise man gratifies every appetite and every passion, while the fool sacrifices all the rest to pall and satiate one.

Henry Fielding

The money of fools is the heritage of great minds.

French proverb

Poverty cannot disgrace the wise, nor can lust enslave them.

Ibn Gabirol

Let me smile with the wise, and feel with the rich.

Samuel Johnson

In our culture we make heroes of the men who sit on top of a heap of money, and we pay attention not only to what they say in their field of competence, but to their wisdom on every other question in the world.

Max Lerner

The wise know the value of riches, but the rich do not know the pleasures of wisdom.

Hebrew proverb

If it be true that a man is rich who wants nothing a wise man is a very rich man.

Jean de La Bruyère

The most certain sign of wisdom is a continual cheerfulness. Her state is like that of things in the regions above the moon, always clear and serene.

Michel de Montaigne

Adversity makes men wise but not rich.

John Ray

Behold, the fool sayeth: "Put not all thine eggs in the one basket"—which is but a manner of saying, "Scatter your money and your attention." But the wise man saith, "Put all your eggs in one basket and—watch THAT BASKET."

Mark Twain

It requires a great deal of boldness and a great deal of caution to make a great fortune; and when you have got it, it requires ten times as much wit to keep it.

Meyer A. Rothschild

A fool may make money, but it needs a wise man to spend it.

Charles Haddon Spurgeon

A wise man ought to have money in his head but not in his heart.

Jonathan Swift

Women

Every man has his price, and every woman her figure.

Anonymous

Women's battle for financial equality has barely been joined, much less won. Society still traditionally assigns to woman the role of money-handler rather than money-maker, and our assigned specialty is far more likely to be home economics than financial economics.

Paula Nelson

There certainly are not so many men of large fortune in the world, as there are pretty women to deserve them.

Jane Austen

A single woman with a narrow income must be a ridiculous old maid, the proper sport of boys and girls; but a single woman of good fortune is always respectable, and may be as sensible and pleasant as anybody else.

Jane Austen

In a society in which money determines value, women are a group who work outside the money economy.

Margaret Benston

Men are foolish, they think money should be taken from the rich and given to the poor. Women are sensible, they think money should bc taken from the rich and given to them.

Richard J. Edham

If one is rich and one's a woman, one can be quite misunderstood.

Katherine Graham

I think people still want to marry rich. Girls especially. . . . (It's) simple. Don't date poor boys. Go where the rich are . . . You don't have to be rich to go where they go.

Sheilah Graham

Where young ladies bring great fortunes themselves, they have some right to insist on spending what is their own; and on that account I have heard the gentlemen say, a man has sometimes a better bargain with a poor wife, than with a rich one.

Henry Fielding

There is only one thing for a man to do who is married to a woman who enjoys spending money, and that is to enjoy earning it.

Ed Howe

It makes no difference what it is, a woman will buy anything she thinks a store is losing money on.

Kin Hubbard

Women prefer men who have something tender about them—especially the legal kind.

Kay Ingram

A woman of fortune, being used to the handling of money, spends it judiciously; but a woman who gets the command of money for the first time upon her marriage has such a guts in spending it that she throws it away with great profusion.

Samuel Johnson

Nothing is more intolerable than a wealthy woman.

Juvenal

The making of money simply is not a sex-linked skill. Women can and are turning it all around. We are discovering for ourselves the challenge—and the joy—of money.

Paula Nelson

The rich woman who marries a money-loving husband is as good as unmarried.

Juvenal

A woman's best protection is a little money of her own.

Clare Boothe Luce

. . . women don't understand these things. They only understand money when they can see it. They're very crude essentially. They don't understand where money comes from or what it means or how a man can be worth money though he hasn't any at the moment. But a man understands all that.

Joyce Carol Oates

Weren't for gold and women, there would be no damnation.

Cyril Tourneur

If women didn't exist, all the money in the world would have no meaning.

Aristotle Onassis

I could not possibly count the gold-digging ruses of women, Not if I had ten mouths, not if I had ten tongues.

Ovid

No woman is ever too slim or too rich.

Mrs. William Paley

Being a woman has only bothered me in climbing trees.

Frances Perkins

We women ought to put first things first. Why should we mind if men have their faces on the money, as long as we get our hands on it?

Ivy Baker Priest

Money and women are the most sought after and least understood things of any we have.

Will Rogers

A fool and her money are soon counted.

Helen Rowland

From birth to age eighteen, a girl needs good parents. From eighteen to thirty-five, she needs good looks. From thirty-five to fifty-five, she needs a good personality. From fifty-five on, she needs good cash.

Sophie Tucker

Work

I cannot afford to waste my time making money.

Louis J. R. Agassiz

There are two things needed in these days; first, for rich men to find out how poor men live; and, second, for poor men to know how rich men work.

E. Atkinson

Money, material though it be, does lie at the base of the most useful work you do. In itself nothing, it is the basis of much of the best effort which can be made for spiritual purposes.

Arthur J. Balfour

For anything worth having one must pay the price; and the price is always work, patience, love, self-sacrifice—no paper currency, no promises to pay, but the gold of real service.

John Burroughs

What's worth doing is worth doing for money.

Joseph Donohue

The law of work does seem utterly unfair—but there it is, and nothing can change it: the higher the pay in enjoyment the worker get out of it, the higher shall be his pay in money also.

Mark Twain

If I wanted to get anything out of this business it was never to have to go back and work in a factory again. But one thing I've learned is that money never buys you out of being working class. The middle classes never let you forget where you've come from.

Roger Daltrey

We reject the notion that the work that brings in more money is not more valuable. The ability to earn money, or the fact that one already has it, should carry more weight in a relationship.

Rosalyn Drexler

If the work you are doing is useful, it will return you a good living.

William Feather

I worked for charity all my life, and now it's kind of fun to work for money.

Charlotte Ford

He that payeth beforehand shall have his work ill done.

Thomas Fuller

It's something I've always wanted to do. I figured I can't ride horses all my life.

Cornelia Guest

I simply don't see the point of getting up at six all the time you are young and working eighteen hours a day in order to be a millionaire, and then when you are a millionaire still getting up at six and working eighteen hours a day . . . What does it all mean?

Nancy Mitford

The way to accumulate money is to keep too busy to spend it.

Arnold Glasow

When a man tells you that he got rich through hard work, ask him whose?

Don Marquis

We are faced with a choice between the work ethic that builds this nation's character—and the new welfare ethic that could cause the American character to weaken.

Richard M. Nixon

We forget what gives money its value—that someone exchanged work for it.

Neal O'Hara

Not to admit poverty is a disgrace—but not to get away from it by work is a greater disgrace.

Thucydides

INDEX